LEGENDS AND FOLKTALES OF LAPPLAND

Legends and Folktales of Lappland

by

VALERIE STALDER

Illustrated by Arnulf Bjørndal

MOWBRAYS
LONDON & OXFORD

© *Valerie Stalder 1972*

Printed in Great Britain by
Alden & Mowbray Ltd at the Alden Press, Oxford

ISBN 0 264 64582 0

First Published 1972 by A. R. Mowbray & Co Ltd,
The Alden Press, Osney Mead, Oxford, OX2 OEG

TO TERJE

Contents

CONTENTS

Foreword

THE folklore of Lappland is rich and varied. But it was kept alive for many centuries by word of mouth only, from one group of Lapps to another. The first person to realise that it might one day be lost, if it were not permanently recorded, was J. Quigstad. He, with several helpers, spent a long time visiting Lapps all over Lappland, listening to the old tales they had to tell—and writing these down verbatim. When he had finished, he collected all the tales together, and put them out in book form.

Each tale was printed exactly as the Lapp who had told it to him had recounted it. No word was changed, added, or subtracted. No attempt was made to render anything in a more readable style than the *extremely* dry one it had been told in. Many of the tales were repetitive, being slight variations on the same theme, from various parts of Lappland. Many others owed their origins to Middle Europe: tales of princes and princesses, etc.—and were therefore not of genuine Lapp origin.

In short, the Quigstad books were a written record of a spoken folklore. Tales painstakingly *collected* by—but not *written* by—Quigstad. And not books for *reading* by a wide public—more for *reference* by a few scholars. I have used this reference material as a *background* for my own stories—which appear in this book. The *background*—and the characters which appear in the stories, such as Stallo, are therefore rigorously authentic. The *foreground*—the action which goes on around these characters—is my own original work. Some of the stories may be slightly similar to the reference material, in certain points. Most of them are not, because they are *entirely original plots*.

In each story, I have attempted to 'explain Lappland' a little, so that those readers who are unfamiliar with the Lapp nomads and their way of life may better understand, and enjoy.

I hope that both those who know and love Lappland, as well as those who have never been there, will like the result.

Tromsø, Norway 1971   VALERIE STALDER

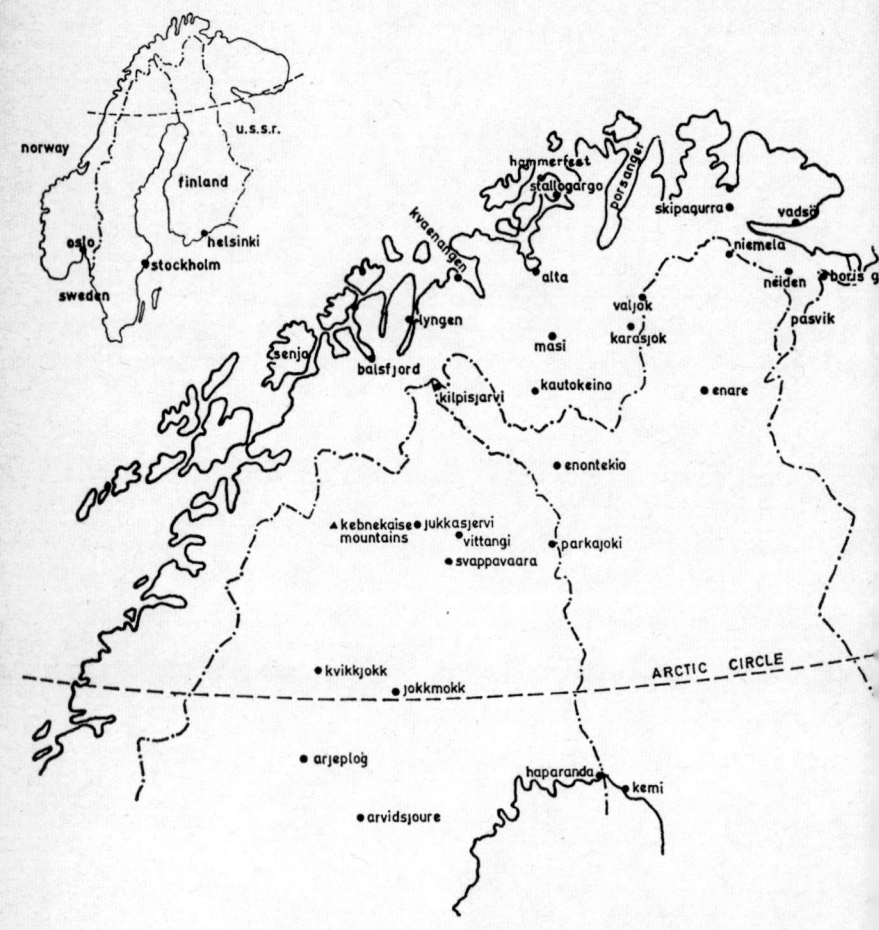

MAP OF THE PLACES MENTIONED IN THIS BOOK

LEGENDS AND FOLKTALES OF LAPPLAND

The angry Northern Light streaked menacingly above,
and struck Biete

1

The Lapp who made fun of the sun, the moon, the stars, and the northern light

ONCE there were two Lapp brothers who lived very far north indeed—near Skipagurra in the Varanger region of Norwegian Lappland. The elder one, whose name was Garrel Uvla, was hardworking, friendly and kind—but the younger one, Biete Uvla, was lazy, rude and rough.

One day in late winter Garrel and Biete went up in the mountains to collect together their reindeer herds. They set off very early, each in his own sledge pulled by a special, trained reindeer—and before the sun rose they had gone a good distance. When he saw the sun, Biete began to 'yoik' (which is the Lapp way of singing)—making up the words as he sang:

> 'The sun is shining—
> Just to bother everything which is cold;
> It makes the snow melt—
> And annoys the ice—'

Hearing this, Garrel said to his brother, 'Biete—do not dare make fun in this way of the heavenly creations.'

But Biete paid no attention to what Garrel said, he just yoiked on, even louder and stronger.

Not long afterwards, the sun he had made fun of covered

itself with clouds—and there came a heavy snowstorm. This made it impossible for them to travel any further; they had to set up their tent where they were, and stay there. Every time Biete looked out of the tent a high wind blew snow all over him. It was several days before good weather returned and they could set off again.

At night, the moon shone clear and bright. Then Biete started to yoik again:

> 'Little moon, little moon—la, la,
> Sitting up there like a fool,
> Trying to shine in the darkness—na, na,
> With you comes the frost,
> Which ruins the work of the sun—ha, ha,'

Garrel was so alarmed that he forbade his brother to say these things—but Biete paid no attention.

Soon the moon he had made fun of disappeared and there came a terrible, thick, dark fog, as they were out in the mountains. And again they had to stay where they were for several days, because they could not see to find the way.

And Garrel said, 'Now you see—you allowed yourself to make fun of the heavenly creations. And so this is what happens!'

At last the thick, dark fog lifted and it was beautiful weather again; so they continued in their search for the reindeer herds. And at night, the stars glittered in the black velvet sky. Then Biete started again to yoik:

> 'The stars are so small—ha, ha,
> They try to sparkle and twinkle—ho, ho,
> And look so stupid and foolish—he, he,'

Garrel tried once again to warn him, saying, 'Stop—some

4

evil will befall you, if you continue to make fun of the heavenly creations!' But Biete would not listen to him.

Shortly after this, not only did the stars stop glittering, but there came a flash of forked lightning, which struck Biete's reindeer, killing it.

Sadly, Garrel said to his brother, 'You are already punished for your carelessness, and for your crazy yoiking. If you do not stop all this immediately, you will see that something even more terrible will befall you!'

They continued on their way—but now Biete had to *walk* through the snow, *and* pull his sledge himself—which before his reindeer had pulled with him riding in it.

In the evening Garrel made a halt, to let his own reindeer rest and eat, and to wait for his brother. He kindled a fire, and began to cook a meal. Just as the food was ready, Biete arrived, looking very badtempered and unpleasant. He joined his brother, and without a word of thanks, partook of the food which Garrel had cooked.

When they had finished eating, they saw that the sky was full of beautiful shimmering Northern Light, which moved and undulated from horizon to horizon. Then Biete started again to yoik:

> 'The Northern Light runs—vip, vip, vip,
> It is greased to make it hurry—bip, bip, bip,
> With a hammer beating it in front—
> And an axe beating on its tail—'

Garrel forbade him one last time, saying, 'Many times I have warned you not to make fun of the heavenly creations. Now I will say no more. You will bring a dreadful fate upon yourself.'

Still Biete would not listen. He yoiked on and on—

louder and stronger. But then the Northern Light began to streak wildly and menacingly across the sky, so that it struck the snow with a bright light and a loud C-R-A-C-K! Garrel turned his sledge over, and crept underneath it for protection. In its fury, the Northern Light struck Biete, killing him, and burning his reindeer-skin coat to ashes. When he saw what had occurred, Garrel drove away with a heavy heart, sorrowing for his brother.

Everyone in Lappland has heard this story. And that is why the Lapps still have this belief: one should NEVER make fun of the Northern Light—because it might get angry and burn one up.

2

The two poor Lapp boys who became herdsmen for an underworld Lapp

ONCE there were two young Lapp brothers whose father was very poor. They were mountain Lapps, who lived in Masi in winter and migrated in spring to the coastal region near Kvaenangen. They only had a very few reindeer, because they were so poor.

One day in springtime, they went together to search for their few animals, which had been grazing untended all winter. They walked and walked—but could not find their reindeer anywhere.

Now a big herd is fairly easy to find—but when there are only a few animals, these can be very hard to spot in the big snowy forests and mountains of the Lappland country. And although the two brothers, whose names were Mikkel Pulk and Hanno Pulk, walked and searched for days, they could not find their animals.

One day when they were very tired, they stopped for a rest. After a meal, and a short sleep under the protection of a jutting boulder, they awoke to see a number of reindeer moving in the valley below. But when they had driven them together, and could examine the brand-mark on their ears, to their disappointment they found that these

7

were not *their* animals. They knew that each reindeer owner has his own brand-mark, so that when the herds wander together during the summer or winter months, they may easily be sorted out at the reindeer round-ups in autumn or spring. And if a Lapp is looking for his own herd in the mountains or forests, he can easily tell whether he has indeed found it—or someone else's herd.

Now, when Mikkel and Hanno looked at the brand-mark on the animals they had found, they were very puzzled indeed. For all the reindeer had a strange mark which they had never seen before! And yet they knew all the brand-marks of the other reindeer owners far and wide! And upon looking about them, they saw that they were in a strange place where they had never been before—although they knew every mountain and valley for many hundreds of miles!

Far off, they could see someone coming towards them—and when he came nearer, they saw that it was a very old man, a mountain Lapp.

He stopped, and said to them, 'Good-day to you—and thank you for collecting together my reindeer—they had wandered away from me.'

Mikkel and Hanno said, 'How strange this is—we do not know you—and we do not know this place. We should be able to recognise every place we come to—but this place we have never seen before! Tell us who you are—and where we are!'

The old man smiled kindly, and answered, 'I am an old underworld Lapp—and this place is an underworld valley. My reindeer had strayed away from me, and now that you have found them, and driven them together, I would like you to stay here, and be my herdsmen.'

Mikkel, who was the younger of the two brothers, answered, 'We cannot stay to be your herdsmen. Our father is a poor man who needs us—and we were looking for the few reindeer he has, when we lost our way. Then we saw your reindeer, and thought they might be ours. But they had not our brand-mark.'

The old underworld Lapp scratched his chin, and then said, 'If you will stay and be my herdsmen, I will give you each a herd of your own—and every single animal shall be *white*!'

Mikkel and Hanno looked at each other in amazement. An entire herd of *white* reindeer—nay, *two* herds? Was it possible? For these were the most valuable animals of all— and very rare—so rare that white reindeer-skins always brought the Lapp trader the highest price, and only a very rich Lapp could afford to have a winter coat made entirely of white skins.

Having thought it over silently, Hanno, the older brother, replied, 'Well—we will stay and be your herdsmen—but we cannot stay forever. Our parents are old and poor, and we cannot leave them. Already, we have been gone so long that they will be wondering what has happened to us.'

So it was agreed.

The old underworld Lapp showed them in which direc- tion to go to find the main part of his herd—and when they had gone some way, they came upon a very large herd, grazing peacefully. There were so very many of them that Mikkel and Hanno could not see where the herd ended— and *every single one of them was white*!

It took the two brothers a long time to round them all up, and drive them back to the place where they had met the old underworld Lapp. After a while, they saw him

9

returning to the same spot—and with him were two pretty Lapp girls.

'These are my daughters', he said, 'and I would like you to marry them. If you do so, I will give you my entire herd of white reindeer between you.'

The two brothers readily agreed to this, for they had not been able to find wives where they lived, being so very poor. And both the old man's daughters were pretty, and friendly.

Soon they were all having a meal, which they cooked in the open, over a birch-wood fire. The girls cooked the food for themselves and their father in *one* pan—and the brothers' food, which Mikkel and Hanno had brought with them, in another pan. When Hanno asked them why they did this, the girls told them that if real Lapps ate underworld Lapps' food, they would never be able to return to the real world.

One day soon after that, just as they had finished eating another meal, the old underworld Lapp said goodbye to his daughters—and suddenly disappeared! Then the two girls told Mikkel and Hanno that it was their father's wish that they should now all return to the brothers' parents. Each girl took one of the leader-reindeer, which every herd has, with a rope and a bell round its neck, the sound of which the others follow—and began to lead the way out of the valley, the entire herd following them, and Mikkel and Hanno bringing up the rear.

They walked for a long way—and all the time the brothers felt as though they were walking in a trance. When at last they came to themselves they were by their father's tent—and their parents were standing looking in speechless amazement at the enormous herd of pure white reindeer!

When the old people saw their sons again, they wept

for joy, and said, 'We thought you were lost forever! Three weeks you have been gone—and although we asked many other mountain Lapps for news of you, none had seen you anywhere.'

They all went into the tent, and warmed themselves at the fire. Then the parents said, 'Tell us where you have been—and where you met these two girls.'

Mikkel and Hanno answered, 'We do not know where we have been, for it was a very strange place which we had never seen before. But we met an old underworld Lapp, who gave us this large herd of pure white reindeer, and his two daughters as wives.'

The next day, Mikkel and Hanno set off with the two girls for a nearby village, one of the few places in Lappland which had a church, to arrange for the weddings. The priest took out a big book, in which were noted the names of all the Lapps for hundreds of miles around. Quite quickly, he found the names of Mikkel and Hanno Pulk—but when the two girls told him their names, he could not find them anywhere in the book, search and research as he would.

So he asked the brothers where they had met these girls—and when he had heard their story he said, 'Now I understand—the names of underworld Lapps are not entered in my book. But before I can marry you, I shall have to baptise them both.'

The girls agreed to this—so the priest took some water and baptised them. Then he could arrange for the weddings.

And so they were married—and were very happy—and had a large herd of pure white reindeer for the rest of their lives.

Sigga gave the big bear a fish to eat

3

The poor Lapp woman and the bear

LONG, long ago, when the Lapps were new on earth, there were some amongst them who practised sorcery. Nowadays, no one knows the secrets of the old sorcerers well enough to use them—but in those olden times there were some families who handed the magic secrets down from father to son, mother to daughter.

Amongst them were Lapps who could change themselves into animals—bears, wolves, etc. Now, a Lapp sorcerer who wanted to become a *bear* knew that he had to go into the woods, and search until he found a tree which had grown with its topmost branches pointing straight to the *north*. Then he had to walk around and around this tree, in the direction of the east, and when he at last became tired, he had to sleep on the east side of it. Before falling asleep, he had to fasten a brush to the back of his clothes—for the tail of the animal he was to become after his transformation. When he woke up, he had to turn again around the tree— but only three times, slowly, and always towards the east. After the third time, he was turned into the bear he had wished to become.

If ever he wanted to turn himself back again into a human, he would be able to do so if he could remember which tree it was he had walked around—and, upon finding it again, turn around it three times slowly, this time towards the west. Then he would instantly become a Lapp again.

And any Lapp sorcerer who wanted to turn himself into a *wolf* had to first search until he found a tree with its topmost branches pointing straight to the *south*. Then, after turning around it towards the east until he was tired, fastening a brush to his clothes, sleeping on the east side, and, upon waking up, turning again three times around the tree towards the east—he would be transformed into a wolf. He too could turn himself back into a human again by finding the same tree, and turning around it three times slowly, always to the west.

Very often, it was the younger sorcerers, those who were learning the magic secrets from their fathers, who wanted to turn themselves into *wolves*—they thought it very exciting to chase the reindeer. Whereas the older sorcerers often preferred to become *bears*, because bears could sleep the whole winter through, and did not have to worry about finding food.

It often happened that the Lapp sorcerer, while he was asleep under the tree of his choice, began to dream of what his life would be as a bear or a wolf. If he had chosen to become a bear, and he dreamed that he was drinking milk, then he would have only good luck as a bear. If, however, he dreamed that he was drinking blood, then he would be killed.

And if one who had chosen to become a wolf dreamed that he had plenty of reindeer to eat, then he would have only good luck. But if he dreamed that he had only stones all around him, then he would suffer from great hunger, and die of starvation.

But, no matter what his dream was, he could not stop

himself changing into a wolf or a bear, once he had got that far. He had to complete the transformation. If the dream had been a very bad one, then the only thing he could do was to try to turn himself back into a Lapp again as soon as possible, before disaster overtook him.

There are many stories told of Lapp sorcerers who transformed themselves in this way—and one of them was told by a poor Lapp woman named Sigga Skalok.

Sigga Skalok was a Skolt Lapp, who lived by a frozen lake near Niemela. One day she went down to the lake and started to fish, after the manner of her people. First she hacked a hole in the ice, and let down a piece of string with bait on a hook. Then she knelt on the ice, and pulled the string up and down. As the lake was very full of fish she had soon caught a goodly number of fine, fat ones. (Indeed, to this day, the Lapps still fish by the same simple system, and still catch many good fish.)

When she had caught enough, Sigga returned to her one-room peat hut, cut some fuel for firewood, and made a fire between the fire-stones in the middle of the floor. Soon she had a brisk fire going, and could cook the fish she had caught. They tasted very good, and she was pleased with her meal. When she had finished, she let the fire down to a glow, and lay down near it to sleep a little. Suddenly, the door-flap was pushed open, and when she looked up in surprise, she saw a huge bear-paw stepping over the entrance. But Sigga was not at all afraid at this—she just said to herself, 'I wonder who this is who has come to visit me today?'

In came an enormous bear, whose fur was completely covered in a thick layer of ice. He turned to the fire, and began to try to warm himself.

Then Sigga said to herself, 'This is not a real bear, but must be one of the Lapp sorcerers who has turned himself into a bear.'

So she put more wood on the fire, to help him thaw himself—and when the thick ice on his fur had melted she cooked some of the fish which she had caught, and had been keeping for herself for the next day, and gave it to him to eat. He was very, very hungry, and ate the fish with grateful enjoyment. When he had finished it he was very tired, and lay down to sleep on one side of the small peat hut. Sigga lay down to sleep on the other side, and slept very soundly, in no fear of the bear.

When morning came, and they woke up, kindly Sigga gave the bear food again, of the little which she had. When the bear had finished, he stood up, and went out of the little hut. Then he stood still, and looked back again. He lifted up the door-flap, and beckoned to Sigga to come outside.

She was not at all afraid, but just thought to herself, 'There must be something he wants to show me'. So she went out of the hut to see what it was. Then the bear showed her the traces in the snow of the way he had come the night before—and waved his paw in that direction to show her that she should follow these traces. Then he went on his way, in another direction.

Sigga followed the traces in the snow—and, after walking for a while, she found a big bear, lying dead in the snow. She returned to her peat hut, and thought about what she had found. When her husband came back from the mountains, where he had been tending his few reindeer, she told him all about the bear's visit—the traces in the snow which she had followed—and the big, dead bear which she had found.

Her husband went out, and followed the same traces until he came to the dead bear. He skinned the bear—and underneath the thick fur he found a purse full of money—more money than he had ever seen in all his life!

The following summer, Sigga and her husband went down to a small Lapp village some distance away, to attend the market which was being held there. They met many friends to exchange gossip with—friends whom they had not seen for several months, as the nomadic Lapps live in lonely places all over their widely-spread country.

Suddenly, a very big man separated himself from the group he was among, and came over to Sigga and her husband. He greeted them politely—and then thanked her because, the winter before, she had taken care of him, thawed him when he was frozen, fed him when he was hungry.

Then he asked Sigga, 'Did you find my dead brother?'

'Yes, we did,' she answered.

'And did you find his purse?' the man went on.

'Yes, we found that too. And now it shall be returned to you, his brother.'

'Oh no!' said the man, 'I wish you to keep the purse, and all the money in it, for you are the one who was so good and kind to me when I needed it most. And you will find that the money in that purse will never run out. It will always be full whenever you need it.'

So poor Sigga Skalok was well rewarded for her kindness.

4

The little boy who was stolen by underworld Lapps

In the spring, the mountain Lapps who own reindeer herds drive their animals down from the winter pasture grounds in the mountain forests, to the summer pasture grounds on the coast.

One year, a group of Lapp families was on this Great Trek (as it is called)—and amongst them was a young couple, Jossa Rias and Elen Rias, who had a little three-year-old son called Husi. They started from a place high in the Kebnekaise mountains in Swedish Lappland, and after a three-weeks journey they came to a place which was only a short distance from the coast. Here they set up their tents to take a day's rest, and also to rest their animals. And little Husi ran in and out of the tent, playing nearby, just as he usually did.

The next day everyone was very busy—taking down the tents and packing them on the sledges—loading the food and the cooking utensils—rounding up the reindeer herd which had been guarded by two herdsmen during the night—and putting between the shafts the reindeer which were trained to pull the sledges.

No one had time to watch little Husi. And he went out

of the tent—and did not come back. Suddenly his mother, Elen Rias, noticed that he was not there and went to look for him. But she could not find him.

She asked the menfolk, 'Has my little boy been near here?'

'We have not seen him,' they answered.

Her husband, Jossa Rias, then said, 'Did you not have time to go and look for him when he first went out of the tent?'

'No,' she answered, 'I did not have time. I had so much to do with packing our food, and the pots for cooking, the reindeer skins we sleep on—and so many other things. And you know that he often runs in and out of the tent, but always comes back.'

Then she went to the herdsmen who were busy with their reindeer, and asked 'Have you seen my little son?'

'We have not seen him,' they answered, 'and we have had no time to see anything but our reindeer.'

And so Elen went further around to look for him, wondering wherever he could be, for such a small boy would not wander out into the wilds on his own.

Not far off were some other mountain Lapps, and soon Elen reached the place where they had their tents. They helped her look for Husi, saying, 'Perhaps he has fallen asleep behind a dune.'

But although they searched and searched, he was nowhere to be found.

Now, amongst these other Lapps was an old, old woman—and she told Elen, 'If such a little boy is lost, and you really cannot find him anywhere, then it can only be that the underworld people have stolen him. And you will not find him by further searching. And all the time you have been looking for him, your people have been preparing to leave this place, for they must reach the coast today, before the reindeer start to calve. And now they are ready. You cannot delay them any longer. But someday, somewhere, you will be given some sign as to how you can get your little boy back again.'

Elen went back to her husband, and told him what the old woman had said. And then, very sad at heart, they continued on their way with the rest of their people and their herds, until they came to their summer place near Hellemo, on the Norwegian coast.

About two weeks later, Jossa Rias had a strange dream. He dreamed that a voice said to him, 'In autumn, when you return with your reindeer to the winter pastures, put up your tent again near the place where your little son disappeared. When you lie down to sleep, turn your face to the west and your back to the east—and then perhaps you will find him again.'

When he woke up, and told Elen of the dream he had had, she only said, 'But how can *this* help us to find our little boy, who was stolen by the underworld people?'

'I do not know,' Jossa replied, 'that was not spoken of in my dream.'

Some time later, Elen Rias bethought her of an old Lapp witch-woman, who lived nearby in Hellemo. So she went to see her—and told her of all that had happened, and of the dream which her husband had had.

'What does it mean—and what should we do?' she asked.

The old woman thought awhile, and then said, 'I cannot tell you anything today. I must think of what the meaning could be. In three days time, you may ask me again.'

So three days later Elen returned—and this time the old Lapp witch-woman was able to tell her, 'You had put up your tents right beside an underworld tent—and it *was* the underworld people who stole your little boy. They did it because they have no sons of their own, only daughters. They have him in the first sand dune east of where you had you tent. But if you do as I shall tell you, you may be able to get him back again.'

Elen listened very carefully, as the old witch-woman went on to say, 'In autumn, when you return to that place with your herds, set up your tents three miles from where you had them in spring. You yourself can do nothing to find your son, for he was stolen by an underground woman, from a household where there are women only—and he, who is male, can only be taken from them again by a male. So you should sleep in your tent as usual. But your husband should go, as soon as darkness falls, to the sand dune I told you of—and lie down nearby, with his face to the west, and his back to the east. Then, being near the place where they are keeping your little boy, if he happens to see him, he must approach him *backwards*—and seize him from them *with his arms behind his back*. When he has him, he must hold him firmly, and hurry back to your tent. In the morning, you should leave the place—and never set up your tents there again.'

Elen thanked the old Lapp witch-woman for her advice, and hurried home to tell her husband.

When autumn came, and it was time for the reindeer to return to the winter pasture lands in the mountains, Jossa and Elen Rias rounded up their animals and set off. They put up their tents three miles from the place where they had had them in spring.

When darkness at last fell, Elen remained inside their tent, and Jossa walked until he found the first sand dune to the east. He lay down nearby, with his face to the west, and his back to the east. He strained his eyes for any movement—and his ears for any sound. After a long while, he saw two Lapp underworld women walking nearby—and between them was his little boy, Husi! Silently, in his skin boots, he approached them backwards, looking over his shoulder to see the way. He stretched out his arms behind him—and when he was near enough, he seized little Husi! Then he turned and, holding his son firmly in his arms, he ran swiftly back to the tent.

Husi's mother was overjoyed when she saw her son again, and happy tears ran down her cheeks.

'Where have you been—oh, where have you been?' she asked, clasping him to her. But little Husi could not tell them. He still had on the very same clothes he had been wearing on the day he vanished. But when his mother looked at them more closely, she found that all the pockets were full of gold coins!

In the morning, the whole family moved on, with the rest of their people—and they never set up their tents on that spot again, although they came back the same way many times, as each year brought another spring—another autumn.

And with the gold coins, they bought many reindeer, which they added to the herd which belonged to Husi. Each animal was branded with Husi's own brand-mark—and when he grew up he had a fine large herd to be proud of.

5

Hidden treasure in Lappland

In the old days, those of the mountain Lapps who owned many reindeer, and had become rich from the trading and selling of both animals and skins, used to bury their money in the ground. They put the money either in an old metal cauldron (the kind they did their cooking in) or in a heavy, wooden box. Then they dug a deep hole in the ground and put the cauldron or box in it, as far down as possible. Next they put birch-bark over and all around the hole, and then slabs of stone around that, with a big stone on top onto which they carved their name with a knife. Finally, they covered the whole thing with earth and sand, to disguise their hiding place.

Now, if the Lapp who buried the treasure died, or chanced to get killed, before digging it up again, and, because no one else knew of its hiding place, it was left to lie buried for a long time, undisturbed, they say that it would often start to *burn* and that on Midsummer Night flames even came up out of the ground, over the place where it was buried.

If anyone chanced to pass by the spot, and saw mysterious flames coming up directly out of the ground, he should turn his eyes away, and hurry from the place. If he did not do so, but instead tried to dig out and steal the buried money, only evil would befall him and his family for several generations. This everyone in Lappland knew.

But of course there are always dishonest people everywhere who think *they* know better—and of such people the following story is told.

Once there was a rich Lapp sorcerer who buried all his money high up in the mountains near Kilpisjärvi, where Norwegian, Swedish, and Finnish Lappland meet. Now when a Lapp sorcerer buried a treasure in this way, he was careful to cast an extra specially strong spell over it, to protect it from theft. And anyone attempting to steal it would suffer many unpleasant surprises, and much ill luck.

Many years later, a dishonest Lapp happened to pass that way on Midsummer Night. His name was Bannus Ber, and he was thinking of the many reindeer he had seen grazing without herdsmen—and was planning how he could steal some. This wicked thought was in his mind, when suddenly, at a short distance from where he stood, he saw a place where flames were emerging from the very ground—shooting up—and darting from side to side!

Bannus became very excited, for he knew it could only mean one thing—beneath the flames was hidden treasure! Already thinking of how he would spend the money—he forgot the danger. Quickly he ran to the spot, and threw sand on the flames until they went out. Using a thin, flat stone as a shovel, he started to dig. It took him a long time, but he dug and dug, until at last he came to the wooden box with the money in it. He gloated over it for awhile and then loaded it into the sack which he carried on his back, and took it home to his tent.

Several days later, Bannus went to a rich Lapp who owned many reindeer, and said he wished to buy some for his own herd. The rich Lapp was willing to sell, but when Bannus pulled out the money he had stolen it turned to dust in his hands! For this was money which had belonged to a Lapp sorcerer—and there was a very special spell on it. The person who stole it would never be able to spend it; it would just turn to dust in his hands. And this is indeed what happened. When the thief pulled out another handful of money—the same thing resulted. Even as he held it out in payment—it turned to dust!

Then Bannus became very frightened, for he realised that the money he had stolen must have belonged to a Lapp sorcerer. Now his only thought was to get rid of it as soon as possible, and the only way to be sure that no more trouble would befall him was to return the money to its original hiding-place.

He hurried back to his tent, where he had left the wooden box. His family was very surprised to see him return without the reindeer he had set out to buy. They knew about the money he had found—and when he had told them how it had turned to dust in his hands, they were as frightened as he was. They all agreed that the wooden box must be returned immediately, and reburied.

In his fear, Bannus was shaking and trembling so much that he could hardly carry the heavy box, so his daughter, Berit Ber, had to help him. Together they replaced the birch-bark, and the stones, around the treasure, and piled earth and sand over the top. Then they returned to their tent, and hoped that that would be the end of it. But it was not.

One day, some years later, Berit Ber met a Lapp boy from quite another part of Lappland. His name was Amul Nekela, and he was such a good-looking boy that although

Berit did not know much about him, she soon decided that this was the man she wanted to marry. But the Ber family had only a very small herd of reindeer, and of those only a very few belonged to Berit herself. So Amul was not very eager to marry Berit, because he was hoping to find a Lapp girl with a large herd of her own, to add to his own animals—or at least a girl with the money to buy reindeer.

At last, when Berit feared Amul would leave, and that she might never see him again, in desperation she told him about the hidden treasure. She said that she and her father had buried it—which was true, but only *part* of the truth. She did not tell him that the money had belonged to a Lapp sorcerer, and that there was a spell on it. She hoped in this way first to marry him, and then take him to the hidden treasure by darkness, so that he would not really see the way. Then afterwards, before he could try to spend it, she would return the treasure to its hiding-place, without his knowledge, and so avert any evil in the spell, telling him that it had mysteriously vanished.

Amul was very pleased when he heard of the buried money—and he pretended to agree to the marriage. But, on the eve of the date fixed for their wedding, he told her that he wished to see the treasure with his own eyes, to be sure that it really existed. Berit protested and protested—but to no avail. So, finally, she consented to show him where it was hidden, as long as he promised to leave it there once he had seen it.

They took a shovel with them, and when they came to the place, Amul began to dig. But when he had dug down far enough to see the wooden box, he pretended to be suddenly very afraid. He threw down the shovel, and ran off, crying out loudly of his fear. Berit ran after him, and when she caught up with him, he said to her that it was best to leave the money where it was, for he had seen evil spirits guarding it, who would do them some harm, if they attempted to take it. Knowing as she did that the money had belonged to a sorcerer, Berit believed him, and was very frightened.

They returned together to her father's tent; but later that night Amul went back alone, and carried away the wooden box with all the money in it. His tale of the evil spirits he had seen guarding it was only his own invention—just an excuse to be able to return alone, and steal all the money for himself. So Berit lost the money for a second time— and also lost her faithless sweetheart.

But the money Amul had stolen was to do him no good, as we shall see. He returned with it to his own part of Lappland, and soon there came the day when he wished to buy something with his stolen money. He was one of those Lapps who spend the summer on one of the islands off the coast, which are the summer pasture-grounds for the reindeer. And so he wanted to buy himself a fine new boat, so that he could fish during the summer months.

He found a man who had just the kind of boat he wished for—but at the exact moment of pulling out a handful of money to pay him—he felt a hot, burning sensation in his rear end! It hurt him so much that he began to jump up and down with the pain of it, clutching his rear end with both hands (which was a very funny sight to those watching), and crying out, 'Oh! how it heats! Ow! how it burns!'

For there was still a spell on the money, but the punishment to anyone stealing it was never the same twice— and to him had been meted out the punishment of feeling as though his rear end was afire!

He jumped up and down—around and around—and finally he jumped into the sea, which was nearby, in the hope that the water would put out the flames which he felt sure were burning him. But the sea was much deeper than he had thought, at the place where he had jumped in—and as he could not swim, he was drowned. And so he was punished for stealing the Lapp sorcerer's money—and also for deceiving Berit.

The people standing by soon realised that there must have been a spell on his money, for they saw the wooden box he had left. One of them put it in his boat, rowed it far out to sea, and threw it overboard where the water was deepest. So it vanished, and never did anyone else any more harm.

6

What the months say to each other in Lappland

ANY nomadic reindeer-owner always has one eye on the weather. Whether searching for his animals in the mountains, or tending them during the long migrations in spring and autumn, he constantly watches the sky. A sudden snow-storm in late autumn—or an early defreezing of the lakes which he and his reindeer must cross, in spring, could mean the loss of valuable animals. He must be forever watchful.

And he must bring up his children to be watchful too, so that when their turn comes to lead the migrations, they will know what to look for. During the daytime, he will teach them all kinds of signs to look for and to understand, and ways of avoiding trouble for themselves and their herds as they move through Lappland. In the Far North, the changing months of the year bring the most strange and dramatic changes of climate.

In the evening, as he and his family sit around the embers of their fire, inside their tent, drowsy from their evening meal, the subject of the weather may still be on his mind. And very likely he will start to tell the children the old Lapp tale about the months of the year, and what they say to each other.

'If a mother and father have ten children,' he will begin,

'all twelve of them can talk together as they wish. The eldest can talk to the youngest—the middle ones to both—and all can talk to their parents. But with the twelve months of the year it is not so. Each month can only talk to the month immediately before or after it. And this is what they say to each other.

January: (the second winter month) says, 'I am the first month of the calendar year—but I am not the youngest. The youngest in the family is sister May—but I have never seen her.'

February: (the third winter month) 'I have never seen her either. But I have heard of her from brother March, who had it from sister April.'

January: 'In any case, she has not the beautiful Northern Lights which I have, that flash right across the sky from one horizon to the other, changing from white to yellow—yellow to green—and even sometimes to red—weaving and waving as they go!'

February: 'And she has not my velvet darkness, nor my miles and miles of beautiful, glistening snow-diamonds!'

March: (the lovely-swan month) 'I always wish I was as icy cold as you, February. I would freeze the reindeer to the harness of their sledges, when the Lapp traveller turned his back for a moment! And I would freeze the Lapp women's gloves to the ice, hands and all, when they went to the ice-hole on the frozen lake, to get water!'

February: 'Why don't you do all this then?'

March: 'The sun shines into my eyes; I cannot see enough to freeze things up as I would like to.'

April: (The ugly-crow month) 'When I come along, I *help* the Lapp women to get water for their cooking and washing. I begin to melt the snow, and start the frozen waters flowing again. In the early morning I may be cold—but later in the day I get much milder.'

May: (the spring month) 'When it is my turn, I melt the snow and ice much better than you, April. And I warm up the earth too, all over Lappland.'

April: 'You do your best. And sister June does even greater wonders than you. But neither of you are there to see the wonder which I see—the hundreds of baby reindeer calves which come into the world when I am in the heavens!'

May: 'I see them roaming with the herds on the pasture-grounds by the coast, which I have cleared for them!'

June: (the midsummer month) 'I make the whole of Nature beautiful! When sister May has cleared the way for me, I bring out flowers in the wild country-side, blossom on the berry-plants in the hills, and green foliage on the trees in the forests!'

July: (the summer month) 'I am the warmest month of the year. But sometimes, when I see that the beauties of Nature which sister June has brought forth, are beginning to dry out, I quickly wet them again with rain, so they may stay beautiful.'

June: 'Both of us give whole weeks of light, day *and* night. And by the light of our Midnight Sun, the Lapp children can play, and their fathers can fish for salmon and trout!'

August: (the harvest month) 'I dry out what you, July, have watered. But I ripen the golden cloudberries which little Lapp children love to eat. And I ripen so many of them that their parents can pick many buckets full, all over the country.'

September: (the autumn month) 'I turn the leaves to golden-yellow, deep orange, and glowing red. There are no colours in Lappland as vibrant and lovely as the ones I give to the forests!'

August: 'Yes—but then you make all the leaves fall off—and you weaken the warmth of the sun!'

September: 'I am strong enough to bring out the sweet blueberries, and the red lingonberries—both treats for our friends the Lapps!'

October: (the second autumn month) 'When I come along, I cover the country with a new mantle of white. Just a light one—but enough to make everything pretty again, which you, September, have left so empty and bare.'

November: (the last autumn month) 'But I am the one who makes the world really sparkle and glisten again, under a heavy coat of pure white—whiter than the whitest reindeer-skin coat on the prettiest Lapp girl!'

December: (the first winter month) 'What you have made white, November, I cover with darkness, night *and* day. I take away the sunlight—but I give such beautiful moon-light and starlight for the Lapps to see by. I freeze the rivers, but on the safety of their deeply-frozen ice, the Lapps can drive their reindeer-sledges to the village churches, to celebrate the festival of Christmas.'

January: 'In our own way, each of us does his best to make the world look beautiful. And our friends the Lapps appreciate us all in turn, for what we give them.'

Lapp fathers have been telling this tale for generations. This very night, somewhere in Lappland, little Lapp children may be listening to it.

Many reindeer antlers were offered to the stone

7

The Bring-Luck Stone of Akko

LAPPLAND has many hundreds of miles of flat, wide, open country, often quite barren except for a few shrubs. Here and there, breaking the monotony, one can see a large stone which appears almost to have fallen from the skies. Often, it is quite impossible to tell where it has come from, and as these stones, some of which have been there for centuries, mostly have very curious shapes and lie in weird positions, the Lapps of long ago used to believe that they were put there for a purpose. In the course of time many curious things happened around some of these stones, and many are the legends which have been told, for example, of the Bring-Luck Stone of Akko.

One day, a long, long time ago, a young Lapp and his father were hunting wild reindeer together. All reindeer are branded by their owners soon after they are born— except those few which are born far from the rest of the herd, and which avoid being rounded-up. A Lapp hunter may take any unbranded, or wild, reindeer he can find, for himself. But although Mattis Loso and his father had been hunting for several days, they hadn't seen the slightest signs of any wild reindeer. And now the food they had brought with them was almost finished, so they would soon have to return home, empty-handed.

On this, their last hunting-day before returning, they searched for many miles, and by evening they reached a place named Akko. Mattis was some distance away from his father, and both of them were looking and listening intently. Mattis walked steadily up a bumpy piece of ground to the top of a small hill, which would give him a clear sight all around.

At the top of the hill he found a huge stone—most peculiarly shaped. Never having seen a stone like it before, he stopped to examine it more closely. He walked all around it, surprised at its curious form and position.

Then, remembering his hunting and realising that he was wasting time, he said out loud, 'If only we could find a large reindeer, not just a large stone!'

A few minutes later he heard a shot—and then another. Running in the direction they had come from, he found his father bending over two extremely large wild reindeer. Mattis could scarcely believe his ears when his father told him that these two reindeer had suddenly appeared, within easy shooting range.

'Between them, they will give our family meat for many months—and their fur will go into "pesker" (coats)— "komager" (shoes) and "bellinger" (trousers) to keep us warm!' he added contentedly.

When Mattis told his father about the stone, and what he had said to it a few minutes before, the old man declared that a peculiar stone like that must have been put there for a purpose—and that purpose seemed to be to help wild reindeer hunters.

'The stone sent us the reindeer,' he insisted, 'and it must be thanked. We will give it the antlers.'

Mattis would have liked to keep the antlers, to carve

spoons and other things from, but he did not argue with his father.

When they had skinned the reindeer, cut up the meat, and wrapped the skins around it (to make it easier to carry), Mattis and his father took the antlers of both the reindeer, carried them up the hill, and laid them against the big stone. Mattis' father bowed three times to the stone, and bade his son do the same, whilst at the same time expressing his gratitude for their sudden good luck in hunting. He promised that he would tell other Lapp hunters about the big Akko stone at the top of the hill.

After that many other Lapps came to the stone to ask for help when they were hunting. Time and time again the stone sent them reindeer, and soon it became known, all over Lappland, as The Bring-Luck Stone of Akko.

Mattis' father warned every hunter to remember to thank the stone, by giving it the antlers of the reindeer he shot. This they did—and in time there were so many antlers on, under, and all around the stone, that, many years after it was first discovered, the Lapp hunters decided it was time to give the Bring-Luck Stone something different. So they began to give it hand-carved spoons, and other things which they carved out of reindeer horn, and which they made as pretty as they could, with many different patterns.

The Bring-Luck Stone was always good to those who remembered to thank it. But it took the luck away from those who planned to deceive it.

One day, a Lapp hunter named Heika Gaup went up to the stone and said, 'If you send me hunting luck today, you shall have the antlers of all the reindeer I shoot—and many spoons and cups besides!'

He walked down the hill again—and soon he saw two

reindeer bucks. They were fighting each other furiously, and their antlers were tangled up together. Heika Gaup saw too that one was much bigger than the other, and as he raised his weapon to shoot it, he thought to himself, 'It is *I* who have found these reindeer, and their horns are so tightly tangled together that they cannot possibly pull apart from each other. When I have shot the big one, I shall have plenty of time to shoot the second. And their antlers are so beautiful that I will keep them myself. I shall not give the stone *anything*!'

Exactly as he finished thinking this, the two reindeer suddenly untangled their horns—and vanished instantly from his sight!

Yet another Lapp hunter deceived The Bring-Luck Stone even more. But he was even more punished for it. He was a rich mountain Lapp named Giste Utzi, who owned many reindeer, and he passed the stone when he was migrating with his herd. As he passed it he thought to himself, 'If I could get a new reindeer buck or two, I would give the stone something fine.'

Two miles further on Giste Utzi saw two wild reindeer bucks coming out of the forest, straight towards him. He shot them both, skinned them, and kept the skin, meat, antlers, and all, without giving the stone a single thing. Then he continued on his way, quite ignoring his promise to the stone.

The next year at the same time, when he again passed near the same place, Giste Utzi looked up at the stone, and laughed to himself at the thought of how he had cheated it. Just beyond the stone, in a hollow, he could see what looked to him like a thick, wide patch of low-lying dwarf-birch trees. He was surprised to see this, for there had never been dwarf-birch there before. When he went nearer to have a better look, he found fifty buck reindeer lying frozen stiff and covered by snow. Only their antlers were sticking out of the snow, and these fifty antlers had looked to him like a patch of dwarf-birch trees. And all fifty reindeer were from his *own* herd!

Then Giste Utzi realised that the stone had not forgotten him in the year that had passed since he broke his promise to it.

For many hundreds of years, Lapp hunters continued to give antlers, and small objects carved out of reindeer antlers, to The Bring-Luck Stone of Akko. And although gradually the Lapps stopped believing in the stone, and it lost its power, the antlers and horn spoons are still there. They have sunk below the surface into the peat, pressed down by the winds and storms of changing seasons—but they are there. Mostly they have broken up into small pieces—except for a few of the spoons.

But, wordlessly, they still mark the place of what was once the well-known Bring-Luck Stone of Akko.

8

The shaman Parak-Mikkel
from Enontekio

LONG, long ago, there were many different kinds of sorcerers amongst the Lapps—but the Lapps did not call them 'sorcerers', they called them 'shaman'. There were so many kinds of shaman that the Lapps gave them different names, all according to the powers which they possessed.

One kind was the 'seeing-shaman'; these could *see* all kinds of things and events, often before they happened. They could also see who had stolen anything that was missing, and where it was. Another kind was the 'knowing-shaman'; these were more powerful, because they *knew* everything, even how to make themselves invisible, or how to change themselves into animals. A more powerful kind still was the 'eating-shaman', who could kill his enemies at a distance, or make their reindeer disappear, or conjure up all kinds of dangerous things out of nowhere. When anything like this happened to one Lapp, the others said that a shaman was trying to 'eat' him, and that is why this particular kind of shaman was called, in time, an 'eating-shaman'.

Very few were the shaman who had *all three* of these different powers. Those who did were the most powerful of all, and they were called 'flying-shaman', because they were so powerful that they could even be in several different places at once. And of one of these flying-shaman, a Lapp named Parak-Mikkel, many stories are told. He lived near the Lapp village of Enontekio, in Finnish Lappland, and people were very afraid of him.

One day, he sent his son to the market, to sell a large amount of reindeer meat. Before the son left, Parak-Mikkel said to him, 'Tonight you will sleep in Enontekio. You may safely leave your sledge in the market-place, with all the reindeer-meat on it. Sleep peacefully, for I promise you that no one shall be allowed to steal the meat during the night. But nevertheless, when you return to the sledge in the morning, you will find there someone who *tried* to steal from it. His hand will be frozen to the meat he wanted to steal. Hit him on the hand three times—then let him go.'

The son set off that evening, and when he came to Enontekio, he drove his sledge to the market-place. There he unfastened his reindeer, and led it to a place where it could graze in the night. His loaded sledge was left untended all night, but he slept peacefully, remembering his father's words. In the morning, when he went back to the market-place—there, sure enough, was a man standing with his hand frozen to the meat.

'Aha—you should not try to steal meat which belongs to Parak-Mikkel!' said the son. Then he hit the thief's hand three times. With a cry of pain, the thief jumped away from the sledge, for the three blows had freed his hand, and ran off.

The son let him go, and when he had sold all his reindeer meat, he returned to his father's tent.

'Everything happened as you said it would, father,' he said.

Parak-Mikkel laughed.

'I knew it would,' he said. 'I "saw" it all before I sent you!'

Then there was the time that a thief broke into Parak-Mikkel's food reserve, his stabbur.

Almost every Lapp family has a stabbur, where they keep dried reindeer-meat, dried fish, and other food. And the very oldest Lapp tradition of all says that no one should ever break into another man's stabbur and steal from it—except in a case of uttermost, direst necessity.

Very often, a stabbur is a small wooden hut, but Parak-Mikkel had made a special stabbur of his own, because he wanted to hide not only food, but also money. His stabbur was in the top of a tall, thickly-foliaged fir tree. And he had broken off all the lower branches of the tree, and made the trunk smooth and flat, so that no wolverine could climb up it and steal his food.

One day, when Parak-Mikkel had been away for a long time in another part of Lappland, he came back to find that someone had broken into his stabbur. Most of the food was gone—and all of the money. This made him very angry; and he was all the more angry because, at the time of the theft, he had been so very far off, and thus had not been able to 'see' what would happen. Even his 'knowing' powers were rather weak about it.

But, after thinking for some time, he finally said to himself, 'I "know" that this thief has already been punished for his theft, by being unable to *cook* the food he stole from me. For him, no fire will light under it. And by tonight, I shall know his name!' He went back into Enontekio, and waited. And by nightfall, rumours had reached him of strange things happening to one of the village Lapps.

For the past two weeks, this man had not been able to

cook any hot food. Every time he lit his fire, between the fire-stones on the floor of his tent, it went out again. He had brought in dry wood, and dry birch twigs to start the fire with—but out it went again each time, soon after he had lit it. No matter how often he tried, and how desperate he got—the fire just would *not* stay lit.

No one could understand it—except Parak-Mikkel! The shaman did not hurry to the man at once; he waited another two weeks, until the thief had been eating cold, uncooked food for a month. Then he went to see him.

'Are you not ashamed to steal from a stabbur?' he asked sternly.

The thief looked startled.

'But—I—I—' he began.

'Oh, it was you all right,' Parak-Mikkel went on. 'I "knew" it soon after I came back and found my stabbur plundered. But *you* did not know that it was *my* stabbur you had stole from!'

By now the thief was thoroughly frightened.

'You will never get your fire to light until you have returned everything that you stole from me and half as much again, both of food and money, to punish you for the greatest dishonesty a Lapp can show—stealing from another Lapp's stabbur,' Parak-Mikkel told him. 'Until you have done that, you will have to go on eating cold, uncooked food.'

Then he went back to his own tent.

In a very short time, the thief returned as much food and money as he had stolen—and half as much again. For he had not stolen from poverty, just from greed. And only then would his fire burn, and cook his food.

On yet another occasion, Parak-Mikkel showed a group

of Lapp families his shaman powers. He was in the woods one day, cutting fuel, when he heard the bells of a large herd of reindeer nearby. He knew that these must belong to three Lapp brothers who kept their herds near Enontekio in winter. They must have just got there that same day, and as Parak-Mikkel knew that they always set up their tents near where he had been cutting wood all day, he put on his skis, and went to see them.

The women were busy in the tents, and the men were seeing to the reindeer. In all the tents, reindeer-meat was cooking in the big, heavy pots on their long chains over the open fire between the stones. The fragrant smell of it made Parak-Mikkel feel suddenly very hungry, for he had been working hard all day. The only thing he had with him was a little bread.

'Have you a small piece of meat you could sell me?' he asked one of the women. 'I don't need much—just enough to make some thick meat-soup.'

The woman looked at him and said, 'I have no meat to sell you. I have not much meat for myself, let alone for others.'

Parak-Mikkel went to the other women in the other tents, and asked if they would sell him a small piece of meat. All of them gave the same answer as the first one had done.

He was not only hungry, but he was also tired, so he asked if they could find some room for him in one of the tents. Grudgingly, they agreed. When their reindeer-meat was cooked, all of them ate plenty of it, licking their fingers and smacking their lips over it. But still they did not give any to Parak-Mikkel, who had to be content with his dry bread.

And in this they broke the old Lapp tradition of always

sharing everything with any stranger who needed the hospitality of another's tent. They should not have treated *any* Lapp in that inhospitable way; and they would certainly not have done so if they had known that their unexpected guest was a shaman, and a very powerful one.

In the morning, Parak-Mikkel was hungrier than ever.

'Can I not buy just a small piece of meat from you? It is quite a long way to my own tent—and I have to carry back all the fuel which I cut up yesterday. I do not want you to *give* me the meat—I will *buy* it from you, and pay for it now, with this money.'

But still they all said, 'We have no meat for you.'

He looked round at them, and as he left he said, 'The next time I come here, I can promise you that you will all have more than enough meat for me. More than I can eat—*or* carry away with me!'

Soon after he had gone, there came a flock of wolves—although before there had not been the slightest sign of wolves that winter. They appeared suddenly, killed forty of the best, fattest reindeer, and then disappeared as suddenly as they had come, without stopping to eat the reindeer.

The next evening, Parak-Mikkel went back again to the same Lapps and their tents. When he got there, he asked, 'And now—do you have meat now—more meat than you know what to do with?'

Then they all realised that it was their guest of the night before who had sent the wolves which killed their reindeer. And they were very frightened, for they knew he must be a shaman. They were afraid that he might send more wolves, to kill all their reindeer—so to appease him they invited him into one of their tents, and fed him with the best pieces of reindeer-meat, and the biggest, most succulent, marrow-bones. Then they prepared a large and comfortable place for him to sleep.

And in the morning, when he left, they gave him as much reindeer-meat as he could carry in a large sack on his back, and would have given him more, if he had been able to take it.

So, in one way and another, a number of different Lapps learned to be very careful when they crossed the path of a shaman—especially if he chanced to be such a very powerful one as the shaman Parak-Mikkel from Enontekio.

9

The Stallo that Rasmus sent
to fight Isak

MANY hundreds of years ago, when the Lapps still practised odd customs which have long since died out, there were times when one or other of them would call into existence a strange being known as a 'Stallo'. This only happened when one Lapp, for some reason or other, quarrelled with another. When this occurred, he threatened the other with the words, 'Beware! I shall send you a visitor!'—always uttered at the end of the quarrel, as he left the other's company. The 'visitor' he meant was a Stallo, whom he would send to fight and kill the one with whom he had quarrelled, and to take all his goods of any value.

But first he had to make a Stallo. To do this he had to go out into the open country, far from any Lapp village or group of tents—taking a shaman with him. Then he had to look for a piece of peat-turf on which no human foot had trodden. Out of this he cut pieces of peat, and laid them flat on the ground in the rough shape of a man. This was as far as he could get on his own.

After that he needed the shaman's sorcery to make his Stallo stand up and move. The shaman took in a deep breath—and blew it out very slowly over the pieces of laid-out turf. Then he called out in a loud voice that the Lapp who had placed them there would give the Stallo half his strength, and half his life—as well as giving half of all his money to the devil—if the Stallo would now stand up, and be ready to serve him in the devil's name. At that the Stallo did stand up, and was ready to serve him— above all to fight the man with whom the Lapp had quarrelled.

The way of fighting was always the same. First, the Stallo would go to his master's enemy, and begin to annoy him in small ways. At this time he was invisible to the other, and so he could tip the food from his plate, pour water over his fire, or hide his skis, all without being seen. After a while the Lapp would realise that all these things were happening because someone had set a Stallo onto him.

Then the Stallo would go away for a while—soon returning, however, to annoy him in more and more ways. This would be repeated over and over again for quite a long time.

Then one day the Lapp would hear the Stallo *whistle*. This whistling was a sign that the Stallo would soon take clear shape, and to the Lapp who heard it, the whistling was full of hidden threats.

Soon afterwards, the Stallo appeared in front of him, and was clearly visible to him. And at once the Stallo would say that he meant to fight the Lapp—and they would agree on an exact day and place for the fight. If the Stallo won he would take all the Lapp's goods, and bring them back to his master. But if the Lapp won, and killed the Stallo, he would take everything the Stallo had. For the Stallo was keeping all the money which his master had promised to the devil, until he could take it to 'Ancient-

Erik', which was one of the names which the Lapps gave to the devil. And if the Lapp killed the Stallo who had been sent to fight him, then the other Lapp who had sent him would fall ill immediately—for had he not given the Stallo 'half his life'? When the Stallo was killed, he took this half with him.

Many are the stories of quarrels amongst the Lapps, and of the fights with Stallos which resulted. And amongst them is the story of Isak Barfi, and the Stallo which Rasmus Gargo sent to fight him.

One day in autumn, Isak Barfi went up into the mountains near Hammerfest, to hunt for wild reindeer. The first day he walked and walked until he was well into the mountainous country where he might expect to find wild reindeer. Late in the evening he stopped, and put up his tent. He lit a fire to cook his food—and when it was ready he ate it with a hearty appetite, for his long walk had made him hungry. He had almost finished eating when he heard the sound of someone approaching his lonely tent. Putting his head out through the door-flap, he saw that it was another Lapp, a man called Rasmus Gargo, also from the region near Hammerfest.

Now Rasmus Gargo had always been of a quarrelsome nature, so Isak was not at all pleased to see him. But, when Rasmus asked if he could share his tent for the night, Isak did not refuse him, for he did not want to break the Lapp tradition of never refusing hospitality. So Rasmus came inside the tent, and cooked his food. Then they both slept. In the morning, Rasmus suggested that as they were both hunting in the same district, they might as well hunt together. Unwillingly, Isak agreed.

On the first day they found no wild reindeer at all.

They returned late to the tent, ate, and slept.

The next morning, Rasmus said that they should make an agreement about their hunting. Whatever they caught should be shared equally between them. He said this because he feared that Isak was the better hunter, and to share equally with him would be to his own advantage. But Isak was afraid that Rasmus might be a better hunter than *he* was—so he agreed to the suggestion, thinking that he couldn't lose by it.

All autumn they hunted together, up in the mountains, and on the day when they decided to return to Hammerfest, they counted the number of wild reindeer they had caught. Isak had found nineteen—whereas Rasmus had found only eleven.

Isak was very annoyed with himself that he had agreed to Rasmus' suggestion about sharing their catch equally—for he now saw that he was by far the better hunter, and that Rasmus had only taken advantage of him.

'I think I should be able to take at least two more reindeer than you take,' he said to Rasmus, 'seeing that I found so many more than you did. That would still give you more than you hunted yourself.' But Rasmus would not hear of it.

'Our agreement was to share everything equally,' he answered greedily.

'I would have done better to stay on my own, and to hunt on my own,' said Isak angrily. 'Then I would have been able to keep what I was able to hunt!'

Rasmus looked up threateningly over the knife he was using to skin the reindeer. Seeing the black look in Rasmus' eyes, and knowing his quarrelsome nature, Isak quickly knocked this dangerous knife out of his hands. Rasmus scowled more than ever—but he let the knife lie where it was.

'Beware—I will send you a visitor!' he shouted to Isak, who was already leaving for Hammerfest to get help to carry his share of the meat and skins down from the hunting-place.

Soon after that there was a heavy fall of snow, and the earth was too hard and frozen for Rasmus to be able to cut out pieces of peat-turf and make a Stallo. But all winter he plotted over it, and in late spring, when the earth was sufficiently thawed again, he hastened into the open country, taking a shaman with him.

Soon afterwards, Isak began to be plagued by any number of annoying things happening, which he couldn't explain. The axe he used to hack wood with disappeared. His cooking pot fell off the chain, and tipped his food into the fire. His skis fell over, and one of them broke. At last he realised that Rasmus must have set a Stallo onto him.

Then one day in summer, when he set out to do some fishing, he suddenly heard someone whistling behind him. When he turned around, however, there was no one there. Further on, he heard the same whistling again, but this time near beside him. Still no one was visible. But now Isak realised that it was the Stallo who was whistling—and that when he heard him a third time, he would be able to see him.

A little later on, he heard the whistling yet again, this time straight in front. And when he looked in that direction, he could see the Stallo at last—waiting for him. And at once the Stallo wanted to settle a time and a place to fight.

'Today I have no time,' said Isak, 'for I am going fishing. But tomorrow at the same time, I will meet you at this same place.'

The Stallo agreed to this—and so the next day they met to fight. The Stallo was strong, and very cunning—and the

E

fight was a hard one. Things went very badly for Isak at first, but after a great deal of effort, he at last managed to get a grip on the Stallo's wide belt. First he forced him down on one knee—then, at last, flat on the ground.

'Do not kill me with your Lapp knife,' cried the Stallo, 'use *my* knife, for mine is of silver, and much better than your rusty one!'

But Isak knew that if he took the Stallo's own knife, it would turn against him, and kill not the Stallo, but himself. So he took his own knife to put an end to the wicked Stallo. Then he took the money which the Stallo had in his pocket, and which was his just reward for defeating him in fair fight.

And on the same day he heard that Rasmus Gargo had suddenly fallen very ill. When the Stallo was killed, he took half of Rasmus's life with him.

And the place where they fought is still called 'Stallo-gargo' by the Lapps. If you look carefully on the map you can find it.

'*Don't you see what is stuck to my foot?*' yelled Stallo

10

Stallo and Luttak

THERE were two kinds of Stallo in ancient times in Lappland. One was the kind which was made by a Lapp and a shaman out of pieces of peat-turf. And the other kind was made out of the *Lapp himself*.

All he had to do was to find a cave or large hole, in the side of the biggest mountain near where he lived—and go there on the last day of any month. Then he promised half his money to the devil, in return for the power to make himself invisible whenever he wanted to. Some Lapps, but not all, also asked for great strength and cunning, in return for half their life.

There was once a Lapp who changed not only himself, but also his wife, into the likeness of a Stallo. After that they were always known as 'Stallo and Luttak'. They had not asked for strength or cunning, but just for the power of making themselves invisible. And, as a matter of fact, both of them were very stupid. So much so that almost everything they did went wrong.

One day this Stallo was walking near a lake, when he chanced to see a Lapp who was just beginning to fish there. At the time, Stallo was visible, so when he went up to the Lapp the latter had no difficulty seeing him—and he knew it was Stallo.

'I will bet you that you cannot catch seven different kinds of fish before I do,' said Stallo.

The Lapp, whose name was Jousep Rias, looked up at him.

'And what will you give me if I win?' he asked.

'All the money which I have hidden in my tent!' answered Stallo rashly.

'Then I accept the bet,' said Jousep. 'Let us start at once.'

He took out a fishing net which he had with him in a basket, and he let the net down through a hole which he hacked in the ice. Then he went over to the other side of the lake, to make another large hole, and throw stones into the water below to frighten the fish on that side over to the side where he had his net.

Stallo, who thought that Jousep had gone away and forgotten about his fishing, spent a long time making a set of fish-hooks of different sizes, which he hung on a piece of twine. He was just going to let them all down through another hole in the ice, when Jousep came back, and pulled up his net. Inside it there were so many fish, that when Jousep had laid them side by side, and sorted them all out—he found that he already had seven different kinds of fish!

And Stallo had not even *started* to fish! So Jousep won the bet, and Stallo had to go back to his tent, fetch all the money he had hidden there, and give it to Jousep.

Stallo's wife, Luttak, was very angry with him when she heard about it, and grumbled at him for a long time. So, several days later, Stallo thought that he had better do something to put his wife in a better humour. He set off again, and out in the open country he came across a little Lapp boy who was playing with his lasso. When the little boy saw Stallo, he was at first afraid.

'What are you doing, out here all on your own?' asked Stallo.

The little boy did not answer.

'If you won't answer me, I shall take you with me, and put you in my cooking-pot!' threatened Stallo.

'Take me then—if you dare!' said the little boy suddenly.

Stallo picked him up, and took him back to his wife. Luttak was just cooking supper when he arrived. When he saw the cooking-pot on its chain over the fire, the little boy knew that Stallo meant to put him in it.

So he screwed up all his courage, and began to sing as loudly as he could 'Both my father *and* mother are flying-shaman—and my brother and sister moved an island!' When Luttak heard this, she was very frightened.

'You stupid dumbcluck!' she fumed to Stallo, 'you have stolen the son of a very powerful shaman—whose wife is a shaman too! Not only that, but even his elder brother and sister are already so clever at Lapp sorcery that they have moved an island from one place to another in the sea! Take him back *at once* to where you found him!'

Hurriedly, Stallo took the boy back again.

Then, for several days, he just stayed in the tent—until Luttak told him that she had no food left to cook, and made him go out and fish.

Stallo thought that the lake which had the most fish was one quite a distance away from his tent. So he set off, and when he came to the beginning of the lake, he made a hole in the ice, and started to fish. But he didn't catch anything—so he moved on further down the lake, and made another hole. He caught nothing there either—so he moved on again, and made a third hole. Still he caught nothing. In this way he moved right down the full length of the lake.

When darkness fell, he was at the very far end of the long lake, and there were holes all down the ice—but still he had not been able to catch one single fish in the lake which he had thought was so full of them! Stallo knew that Luttak would be angry with him again.

He started back to his tent—but in the darkness, and as he was very stupid, he took the wrong way, and wandered out onto the ice-covered lake he had been fishing in all day. He walked a long way, until he thought he must be nearly back at the tent. Then he caught his foot in one of the holes which he had himself made earlier in the day—and he fell over. But he was so stupid, that, in the darkness, he thought he had reached the tent, and had fallen over one of the poles near the entrance.

'Why have you let it get so cold in our tent?' he called out to Luttak. 'Put some wood on the fire!'

Stallo heard no answer, so he called out again, 'Where are you? Do you hear what I say?'

Of course there was still no answer—so Stallo got up to go and look for Luttak. When he tried to stand up, one of his feet was frozen into the ice-hole.

Angrily, he cried out, 'Why are you holding one of my feet, and stopping me from getting up?'

Still his foot was held, and he threatened, 'If you do not let go, I shall not go and fish for you again!'

As still nothing happened, Stallo made a tremendous effort —and succeeded in pulling his foot free, not out of Luttack's grasp as he thought, but out of the ice-hole. But a thick clump of ice still stuck to his foot. In the dark he could not see what it was, and he called out, 'What strange thing have you tied on to my foot?'

There was, of course, no answer, so Stallo tried to pull

the strange object off. But he could not dislodge it—so he started to run, and stamp his feet, to try and throw it off that way. But still it clung to his foot. All night he went on in the same way.

When daylight came, he found that he was on the lake where he had fished the day before. But now he could see to find his way to his tent. He could also see what was on his foot—but as he had never before seen a clump of ice sticking to a foot, he was too stupid to realise what it was. All the way back to his tent, he dragged the one foot that was heavier than the other.

When he got back he called out to Luttak, 'A spirit has got me!'

Luttak came running out of the tent, and asked, 'Where have you been so long?'

'Don't you see what is stuck to my foot?' returned Stallo.

'Did you get any fish?' she asked crossly.

Stallo became very angry, and shouted, 'Don't you hear what I say to you?'

'What do you say?'

'Are you suddenly deaf that you don't hear what I say?'

'I say *what* do you say?'

'Don't you see what is stuck to my foot?' shouted Stallo furiously.

Luttak looked down at his foot, and saw that there was something stuck to it.

'What kind of fish have you got there?' she asked. 'You never caught a fish like that before!'

'A fish—you dimwit! Does that look like a fish!' yelled Stallo.

'What is it then?'

'It is quite clearly a spirit!'

'Then *you* are the dimwit, that you catch a spirit from out of the lake! And you can't keep it here in the tent— take it back where you found it!' ordered Luttak.

'*You* take it back—*if* you can get it off my foot,' said Stallo.

'*I* can't take it back, for I don't know where you caught it!' she answered.

'I *didn't* catch it!' shouted Stallo, '*you* hung it on my foot, when I came back to the tent! And I think you hung it on because I came back without any fish!'

'When did you come back to the tent?' asked Luttak.

'I came back when you had let the fire go completely out, and the tent was freezing cold,' he answered.

'It has never been freezing cold in my tent,' she insisted.

While they had been having this long quarrel the sun had come out, and had melted the clump of snow on Stallo's foot. Stallo was so tired that he lay down to sleep at once, and Luttak was also tired, especially from all the arguing, so she lay down too, and slept. And both of them fell into a long, long sleep.

And, as neither Stallo nor Luttak were ever seen again, the Lapps believe that they are still asleep in their tent, some-where near a cave or big hole, in one of the biggest, loneliest mountains in Lappland.

11

The little Lapp-folk of Barbmo

NOT all Lapp familes are reindeer-owning nomads; some of them live in fixed dwellings the year round—often by the sea, where they can make a living from fishing and hunting. Two such fisher-Lapps were Klemet Tonensis and Morten Saba, who lived near Alta, and who fished together in the small boat they had bought between them.

One day in late autumn, as they were repairing their boat which they had pulled up on shore and turned upside down, a heavy cloud seemed to cover the sun, which until then had been shining brightly. But, on looking up, Klemet and Morten saw that it was not a cloud at all, just a large flock of birds which was flying across the sun, towards the South.

'Look, the birds are already leaving the North!' said Klemet, shading his eyes against the sun.

'Yes, they are flying south to a warmer climate,' agreed Morten. 'Every winter they fly to the land of Barbmo.'

Once the birds have started their migration other birds quickly follow, for all of them feel the increasing cold of approaching winter. And every day after that, Klemet and Morten saw another flight of birds—wild ducks—wild geese—starlings—and many others, leaving Lappland for the warmth of Barbmo.

As soon as their boat was repaired, they started fishing again, but their catch was never very big. Gradually they began to go further and further afield—more and more out into the open sea.

On one such fishing trip, they had already set out from Alta some days before and all they had caught so far had been a very few fish—just sufficient to cook and eat at once, but nothing like enough to take back to Alta. Then, that evening, a heavy wind came up, quite suddenly, and blew their fishing-boat far out to sea. The sea itself was not as rough as one might have expected in such a wind, but it sent the little boat scudding along faster than it had ever moved before, until they were far off their course. This wind kept up for several days and nights, and in all that time Klemet and Morten saw only open sea, with no sign of land anywhere.

Then, one morning, the wind calmed down, the sun came out, and the sky was blue. Klemet and Morten wondered wherever they were! Far off on the horizon they could see something that looked like land—so they started to row towards it. As they got nearer, they could see that it was indeed land; and when they pulled their boat up on the shore, they found that there were so many birds there that they could not even count all the different kinds. Wild ducks—wild geese—starlings—jays—larks—wood pigeons—herons—auks—puffins, all the birds which they had seen leaving Lappland and the North were there on this strange land they had come to!

Before Klemet and Morten had recovered from their astonishment, there was a new surprise for them. Hurrying down to the place on the shore where the two fisher-Lapps had landed, came a number of very little men, none of them much bigger than the birds themselves. Each of them was dressed in Lapp clothing, of the kind worn in summer, without any reindeer-skin coat, leggings or shoes.

'Welcome to the land of Barbmo!', they said to Klemet and Morten. 'You are the first big Lapps ever to set foot here. Only your birds know the way here, because they come to us every winter!'

Then one of the little Lapp-folk added, 'But you are certainly hungry after your long journey—come with us, and you shall eat good food.'

Klemet and Morten followed the friendly little-Lapps, and soon they were all sharing an excellent meal, where there was plenty of both meat and fish. And then the two big fisher-Lapps saw how carefully the little Lapp-folk ate, without ever breaking any of the bones in the meat. So Klemet and Morten were careful to eat in the same way as their hosts.

They stayed for some time in the land of Barbmo, and were able to watch the ways and habits of the little people who lived there. They saw them catch birds with a long pole on the end of which they put a bird-snare which dropped over the bird's neck. But they only snared just enough birds to have sufficient food for their small needs. And they fished too, with nets that they made themselves. They started the netting with a few stitches, which they then hung on two hooks. Then they climbed up and down the netting, adding more stitches each time they went. When they used the finished nets, it took several dozen of them to pull up one net and empty it, if it was full of fish!

And always when they ate, they were very, very careful never to break any of the bones. After eating, they collected

63

all the bones together in a bag, and carried them back to the place where they had caught the birds.

Klemet and Morten liked the friendly little Lapp-folk so much, that they were careful to do everything in the same way as the others did, eating their food with great precaution, and collecting the bones together in a bag, when they had finished. This pleased their hosts so much that they wanted the big fisher-Lapps to stay with them in Barbmo.

But, although Klemet and Morten liked it there, the climate was too warm for them. And besides, they wanted to go back to their own beautiful Lappland, with its wondrous winter snow and skiing through the giant-pine forests; its journeys by reindeer-sledge to visit friends and relations; and its scintillating, undulating Northern Lights, that wonder of Nature.

So at last, when they had been there more than three weeks, they climbed into their own boat again, and set out from Barbmo. All the little Lapp-folk were down on the shore to see them off—and so were all the birds. Klemet and Morten had plenty of food with them for the long journey back to Alta, and their little friends told them in which direction to go.

At last they reached home again—and had a strange story to tell of where they had been.

And every autumn after that, when Klemet and Morten saw the large flocks of birds migrating to the South, they called out, 'Give our greetings to the little Lapp-folk of Barbmo!'

And sometimes, it seemed to them, one of the birds dipped its wings in answer.

12

The Stallo that wanted to marry a nomadic Lapp's daughter

A NOMADIC Lapp and his wife were on the annual spring migration to the coast with their reindeer. They started from the usual place, up in the mountains near Kautokeino. But, that year, they took a different way down to the coast from the way they usually went, because they knew that the way they had always taken before could no longer provide them with enough moss for all their reindeer, now that their herd had grown so much bigger. They had heard that the moss was much more plentiful on the new route.

Unfortunately, however, they did not know this new way as well as they knew the old one—and so they made the mistake of putting up their tent near a Stallo's tent. Usually, the Lapps knew where a Stallo lived, and kept away from the place, but this particular Stallo had only just settled there, so as yet no one knew of his presence.

Now this Lapp and his wife, whose names were Jakup Balto and Marja Balto, had a daughter called Risten. When the Stallo saw the Balto family and all their reindeer, he immediately wanted to get hold of some of these animals for himself. He also wanted a wife to cook and mend for him, so he thought of asking the Balto family for Risten.

Then he would get both a wife, and her dowry of reindeer.

He put on his best clothes, and went to see them. But he still looked like an ugly, wicked Stallo, which he was.

When they heard what he had come for, Risten's father, Jakup Balto, said 'No!'

Her mother, Marja Balto, said, 'No!'

And Risten herself said, 'No—no—no!'

The next day, the Balto family left that place, with their reindeer, and continued on the migration to the coast. But the Stallo came after them, and that evening he again asked for Risten as his wife. And he took out his axe, which he had brought with him this time, and said, 'Unless you do as I want, I will hack you all to little pieces!'

Jakup and Marja were very afraid at these threats, so they pretended to agree to the Stallo's demands, even promising him a number of reindeer as Risten's dowry. But they told him that he would have to come back the next day for his bride, so that they would have time to make her agree to marrying Stallo—and also to give them time to pick out some of their best and strongest reindeer. The Stallo agreed to this, and went away satisfied.

The next day the Balto family did not continue on their way to the coast, but spent the whole day cutting a tree trunk, and fixing branches on to it to look like legs and arms. Then they covered it with their daughter's clothes, reindeer-skin boots and leggings on feet and legs, and put a heavy reindeer-skin coat over everything else. When the Stallo came to collect his bride, Jakup Balto said to him, 'First we will go and look at the reindeer which I have chosen for you and, in the meantime, Risten will make herself ready, and wait for us on her sledge. Then I will drive her to your tent, so that I may know where to visit her.'

While Jakup and the Stallo were looking at the reindeer, Marja laid the disguised tree-trunk in the sledge, pulling the coat up, and the cap down, to hide most of the face part, and draping a scarf over the rest. When the Stallo returned with Jakup, he was thinking so much about the reindeer which he had been given, that he did not look closely at what he thought was Risten on the sledge, and when Jakup said, 'Let us now leave at once for your tent,' he quickly agreed.

When they got to the Stallo's tent, the Stallo went first into it, and Jakup was able to prop the disguised tree-trunk up, near the entrance. Then he went inside and said, 'My daughter is too timid to come in just yet. She is sitting outside, and it may be some hours before she finds the courage to come in. But just leave her there, and in time she will come in by herself. She has also lost her voice for the moment—but she will get it back again.'

With that he left, and hurried back to his wife and Risten, who had already taken down their tent, and packed everything onto the sledges, as well as rounding-up all their reindeer, and attaching the best ones, specially trained, to the sledges, As soon as Jakup got back to Marja and their daughter, the whole Balto family set off again on the migration—and they went as fast as they could, all day and all night, and all the next day, so that they might reach a place where they knew there would be other Lapps, before the Stallo, realising that he had been tricked, could catch up with them.

In the meantime, the Stallo killed one of the reindeer which he had been given, and when he had skinned it, he called to his 'wife' to cook the meat. There was no answer.

'Well, you have lost your voice,' he said, remembering

F

what Jakup had told him, 'and you are timid. This once I will cook the meat—but remember that that is what I got you for, to cook for me!'

He cooked the food, and when it was ready, he called out, 'Come in now and eat!'

When there was no answer, he said, 'Well, stay out there and starve then!' After he had eaten, he called out again, 'Come in, wife, and make up my bed of reindeer-skins for me!'

When there was still no answer, he said, 'This once I will make it up myself. But remember, that is what I got you for, to do things for me, and serve me!'

He made up his bed on the floor of the tent, and then called out, 'Stay out there and freeze, if you want to—I am going to sleep!' And he slept soundly all night.

In the morning, the Stallo was surprised to see that his 'wife' had still not come inside the tent. 'Come in now, and make my breakfast!' he shouted—and when there was not the slightest reply, he got so cross that he rushed out of the tent, seized his 'wife', and shook her angrily.

As he shook, the cap fell off, the tree-trunk rolled over and fell flat on the ground—and Stallo realised that the Balto family had made a fool of him. Furious at the trick which had been played on him, he set out in pursuit of them, taking his big, vicious, black dog with him, to help him.

Now a Stallo who had a vicious dog of this kind was a particularly dangerous Stallo, because in a fight against a Lapp, even if the Lapp defeated and killed the Stallo, he would still be in great danger unless he killed the Stallo's dog too. For if the dog got away, it would bring back no less than *nine* other Stallos—one after the other, to fight the poor Lapp.

But when Jakup had been at the Stallo's tent, he had seen

just such an ugly dog nearby, so he knew that when the Stallo pursued them, he would have to destroy both the Stallo and the dog.

Jakup, Marja and Risten had made such good progress that they had almost reached the place where the other Lapps were, before they saw the Stallo in the distance, chasing after them. Urging his wife and daughter to hurry ahead as fast as they could, Jakup began throwing down pieces of reindeer-meat. When the Stallo's dog found them, he stopped to eat them, gulping them down, hardly stopping to chew. In this way Jakup slowed the Stallo's speed—and into the last piece of meat he pressed a large stone! When it came to this piece, Stallo's greedy dog choked on the stone, which stuck in his throat, and then killed it.

So now Jakup knew that at least there would not be still nine other Stallos to fight.

Marja and Risten had by now reached the other Lapps' tents, and hurried inside, where they found that the Lapp womenfolk there were just cooking some reindeer meat. Soon after, Stallo reached the tents too, and he hurried inside them all, one after the other, to find Risten. But he was not sure what she looked like, never having actually seen her face to face, for he had not spoken directly to either Risten or her mother, but only to Jakup Balto.

Cunningly, he felt the faces of all the women present, because he knew that Marja and Risten had just come in from outside, therefore their faces would be cold whereas all the other women, who had been inside the tents longer, would have warm faces. But Marja had thought of this— and she had rubbed Risten's face and her own with the warm reindeer broth that the meat was cooking in. So their faces were as warm as everyone else's!

The Stallo was more furious than ever when he could not find out which one was Risten. And when Jakup came into the tent, he immediately wanted to fight and kill him. Jakup, who had been busy hacking away some of the ice at a certain part of the lake near where the tents were pitched, at once agreed to fight.

This Stallo was very strong, and he got a grip around Jakup which nearly broke the Lapp's back—but, just in time, Jakup wriggled out of it. Closer and closer to the lake they got, until finally, using every last scrap of energy and strength, Jakup was able to throw the Stallo down onto the ice, just where he had hacked a lot of ice away. Being thin at that spot—and the Stallo being heavy—everything happened as Jakup had hoped. The Stallo fell through the ice, and sank to the bottom. Every time he put his head up—Jakup hit him with a large hammer. Soon the Stallo froze to death in the icy water—which was what he deserved.

And in the Lapp tents where she and her mother had taken refuge, Risten met a young, nomadic, Lapp whom she liked very much.

So when *he* asked to marry her, Jakup said 'Yes!'

And Marja said, 'Yes!'

Whilst Risten herself said, 'Yes—yes—yes!'

13

How Nilas Smukk outwitted Huvva-Mikko

THERE have always been some Lapps who owned no reindeer, and so were not nomadic, but lived in small wooden houses, usually on the shore of a lake, or by the sea. Some of these fixed-dwelling Lapps lived not only by hunting and fishing, but even by cultivating the small piece of land their house stood on. Usually, they did not choose this way of life, but had it forced upon them because they could not buy, nor barter, reindeer.

Owning no reindeer, they had no reason to keep moving —for it is, of course, the reindeer's age-old instinct of migration which forces the owners of reindeer herds to be nomadic. The Lapp follows his reindeer—not the reindeer his Lapp owner. (Except those few which are trained to pull sledges.) Originally, only the very poorest Lapps of all would give up their nomadic way of living in the mountains during the long winter, and on the coast in summer—moving to and from the respective pasture-grounds in spring and autumn.

It was a disgrace for a Lapp to live in a fixed-dwelling. The nomadic Lapp families looked down on those who did so. (And still do.) And any Lapp couple who were unable to make a success of reindeer ownership, felt the disgrace very keenly. If they had children, the children felt it less, for they were born into a fixed-dwelling way of life. But of course they heard their parents speak often of the nomadic, *true* Lapp way.

When they in turn grew up, and had their own children, these were perfectly satisfied with their fixed-dwelling existence—and the stories their grandparents told of their nomadic days even seemed rather strange to them. And by the time the *next* generation of children came along, the family was quite definitely established as a fixed-dwelling Lapp family for all time. But, even so, they always continued to wear the traditional Lapp clothing of their own particular Lapp tribe.

Just such a Lapp family as this was the Smukk family, who lived near Balsfjord. They were a large family—and, in fact, there were so many of them that the small piece of land which they owned was not big enough to feed them all. So three of the brothers went to Porsanger, where they were able to buy a piece of land between them. At that time land was not too expensive—and a rich man in Porsanger lent the three Lapp brothers money to buy enough land, knowing that all three of them were hard workers, and that he could be sure of getting his money back.

Soon after this, Nilas, one of the brothers, went back to Balsfjord to get the horse which the three of them owned together, and to ride it to their new land in Porsanger. After saying good-bye to his parents, sisters, and younger brothers, Nilas set off again with the horse—and rode all day until it began to get dark, which was in the early evening, for this was at the end of August. He found a place where there was plenty of grass for his horse, and made a fire to cook his food on. Then he wrapped himself in warm skins, and lay down to sleep.

The next day he continued, and he rode all day, until it again began to get dark. He again looked for a place where there was food for his horse, cooked his own food over an open fire, and lay down to sleep. But this time sleep would not come to him. He lay wide awake, and just could not fall asleep.

All of a sudden, he saw two men coming towards him. They were dressed in Lapp clothing—and Nilas thought they were nomadic Lapps. But as he did not know them, and he wondered why they had appeared so suddenly and silently out there in such a lonely place, he stood up quickly and took his gun.

One of the approaching men called out, 'Do not harm us! We have not come to harm you—but to help you! We know where you are going, and that your brothers are waiting for you—but unless we help you, you will never get there! For the way you must take will lead you past a place where a dishonest and wicked Lapp has set up his tents. This man was not able to make a success of owning reindeer—but instead of trying to make an honourable living as your great-grandparents did, Nilas Smukk, when they found that the same thing had happened to them— instead of doing that, he has chosen to rob anybody who comes near his tent. All summer he has had his tent at the same place, and he has killed all those who came near, and stolen their money!'

'But perhaps I could go by a different way?', said Nilas, when he heard this. They both shook their heads.

'No, not with your horse. If you were on foot you could take the way you came and went before, but your horse cannot take that way. If you want to reach Porsanger with him, you will have to go past the place where this man is. But—listen to us, and we will tell you what to do.'

Nilas listened very carefully, as they went on to say, 'You must tell him that you are only going to Porsanger to *sell* the horse, and that you are then coming back the same way. This will make him think you have nothing worth stealing now, and, as he has no use for the horse, he will prefer to wait to rob you when you come back, as he thinks, the same way.'

Nilas was very grateful for this advice, and thanked his unexpected visitors for coming. As they left, the two men said, 'It will take you three full days' riding until you reach the place we have told you of. The dishonest Lapp's name is Huvva-Mikko—but before you meet him, you will meet an old Lapp woman who will tell you something else you must do. If you do as she says, you will have good luck on your journey!

When these two visitors had gone, Nilas found that he could sleep at once. The next day he rode all day—stopped when darkness came—and fell asleep as usual. The day after, he set out again, and rode for several hours. At midday, he saw an old Lapp woman coming towards him.

When he reached her, he stopped and greeted her politely, and added, 'It is a pity you are not going in the same direction as I am, for you are old and you look tired. I would let you ride on my horse.'

The old woman looked gratefully at Nilas. Then she

asked, 'Have you perhaps a little dried reindeer-meat which you could let me have? I am on a long journey, and I have but little food with me.'

'I, too am on a long journey—but I will share my dried reindeer-meat with you,' answered Nilas, and gave her what he could.

Then the old Lapp woman said, 'I know where you are going, Nilas Smukk, and that tomorrow night you will come to the tent of Huvva-Mikko. But he will do you no harm if you do as my sons told you. And, to be quite sure that he does not harm you, but only treats you well, I will give you this stone. It comes from the first church that was ever built in Lappland. Place it under the edge of the tent belonging to Huvva-Mikko—but do not let him see you do so. Then you can safely sleep the night in his tent, and he will feed you and treat you well.'

With this, the old Lapp woman gave Nilas a small white stone, and, when he had thanked her for it and for her advice, each of them continued their journeys.

The next day Nilas rode all day, and when it started to get dark he found himself riding along a piece of flat, low-lying ground, wide open on all sides. In the middle of it was a small hill—and on the hill he could see a Lapp tent. At once he knew that this must be the tent belonging to Huvva-Mikko, for its position was such that it gave the owner a good view in all directions, and he could easily see when anyone was approaching.

As Nilas came nearer, an ugly-looking Lapp came down the hill, and waved a stick at him to stop. Nilas stopped, and the man said, 'Good-day!' but very roughly.

'Good-day to you!' answered Nilas politely.

'Where are you going?' asked Huvva-Mikko.

'I am going to Porsanger, to sell this horse,' answered Nilas.

Huvva-Mikko frowned, then said, 'And are you coming back the same way?'

'When I sell the horse, I shall come back the same way,' replied Nilas, diplomatically.

This appeared to satisfy Huvva-Mikko, who then asked, 'Do you want to continue on your way tonight?'

'No, it is dark. I would stay here if there were grass for my horse', said Nilas.

'I will show you where there is grass for your horse, and you can sleep in my tent tonight, and continue tomorrow on your way,' said Huvva-Mikko.

Nilas followed him to a place where he found plenty of grass for his horse; then he followed him up the hill to his tent. Before going inside it, Nilas took the stone which the old Lapp woman had given him, and slipped it under the edge of the tent, as she had told him. Huvva-Mikko gave him food—then made him a comfortable place to sleep, with plenty of warm reindeer-skins. Nilas slept deep and well, and in the morning Huvva-Mikko again gave him food.

As Nilas left to continue on his way, Huvva-Mikko called out to him, 'Be sure and come back the same way when you have sold your horse! I have treated you well, and when you come back, I will prepare a big surprise for you!'

Nilas rode off, and he rode all that day until it got dark. Then he let his horse graze all night again, while he himself slept. The day after, he rode off again, but he had not gone far when he suddenly found himself in a thick fog. He could not see where he was going, but he kept on riding, hoping to get out of the fog.

After a while he came to a place where the fog lifted, and he could see Lapp people carrying hay—and, to his surprise, amongst them were the old Lapp woman he had met on his journey, and her two sons who had come to warn him of Huvva-Mikko. Seeing him, the old woman called to her sons, 'Here he is! Now he and his horse can help us get our hay in!'

'But I have no hay-cart!' protested Nilas.

'I have a big hay-cart,' said the old woman, 'but first— look into the sun!'

Surprised, Nilas looked into the sun—and for a long while afterwards he could not see what was happening. The next thing he knew, his horse was hitched to a big hay-cart and all those whom he had seen were piling hay on top of the cart. Then the old woman jumped on the cart, and told him where to drive the horse and cart to.

When they got there, her two sons and the other Lapps unloaded all the hay, and when it was safely piled up together where she wanted it, the old Lapp woman turned to Nilas, and said, 'Now it is time for us to eat. I would have wanted you to eat with us, but that is not possible. If you eat our food, you cannot return to your own world. For both I and my sons, and all the people you have seen here, are underworld Lapps. We are just the same as you, in every way, but we live in two different worlds. And, even amongst underworld Lapps, there are those who are nomadic, and those who are not. And those whom you have seen here live in fixed-dwellings, as you do.'

Nilas was amazed when he heard all this.

Then the old underworld Lapp woman went on to say, 'When I asked you to give me a little reindeer meat the other day, I only did so to see if you had a generous heart.

For we cannot eat your food, any more than you can eat ours. If I had eaten it, I would not have been able to return to my world. And, for the help that you have given us with your horse you shall be well rewarded. On your way, you will come to a large birch-tree, standing alone, the trunk of which is surrounded by a wide circle of reindeer moss. Lift up the moss—and you will find your reward. But first—look into the sun!'

Again Nilas did as she asked, and looked into the sun. The brightness of it made him shut his eyes—and when he opened them again, he was once more in a thick fog. But he could see where the fog ended—and a Lapp stood there, beckoning to him to ride that way. Nilas rode in that direction, and, when he got out of the fog, the Lapp had disappeared. But now Nilas could clearly see which way he should go.

As he rode along, he came to a place where there was one large birch-tree, standing on its own. And all around the trunk was a wide circle of reindeer moss. Nilas got off his horse, and lifted up the moss. Underneath, he found a bag and, when he looked inside, he found it was full of silver coins. He loaded the bag on to his horse, and that night, when he slept, he let the horse graze as usual, but he tied a rope to it and attached the other end to his foot, so the horse would not stray off.

The next day he rode again all day and in the evening he came to Porsanger, where his two brothers were waiting for him. They listened in amazement to his strange tale of all the adventures which had befallen him on his journey from Balsfjord. Then all three of them looked at the silver coins. And the first thing they decided to do was to repay the man who had lent them money to buy their land.

When they had done that, they sent some money to their parents—and some to their brothers and sisters.

And there was still plenty over to start all three of them off with what they needed for their new land in Porsanger —and to help them take wives, and start families who would grow up to be *proud* that they were fixed-dwelling Lapps.

Eating and resting on their sacks, by the river

14

Two little girls who went to
pick sennegrass

In the winter, when the temperature in Lappland can drop to less than 40° below zero, the Lapps keep warm by wearing many layers of clothing, including trousers, coat, and shoes made of reindeer-skin.

Inside the shoes, they put a thick lining of special grass, with which they pad both the sole and the sides, building it up both under and around the foot in such a way that it keeps the foot completely warm even in the coldest of weather. They use the sennegrass instead of socks—and indeed it is much warmer. When the shoes and grass get wet, both can be dried quickly by the warmth of a fire—and when the sennegrass is old, it can be thrown away and replaced with fresh. Lapp mothers also use sennegrass to line their babies' cradles with. The grass is first beaten against a stone to soften it, and when it is ready, it is both soft and warm for the baby to lie on, and it can be changed as often as necessary, with no trouble.

Although it is used in the winter, sennegrass must be picked in the summer. The Lapp women and girls gather it, beat it to soften it, then plait it up together in thick strands, which they hang up in their tent, or in their stabbur. In winter, they take the strands down as they need them, and unplait the grass for use.

One summer day, two little Lapp girls, whose names were Ravna Siri and Marish Siri, were sent by their mother down to the river near Valjok to look for sennegrass. It grows mostly by the banks of a river, and this particular river had so much of it on its banks that it was even called 'Sennegrass River'.

Their mother had no time to go with them that day, so Ravna and Marish set off on their own, each carrying a sack to put the sennegrass in. They were old enough to go on their own—Ravna was eleven, and Marish was two years older.

It was a beautiful sunny day, and they wandered happily along beside the river, singing and cutting sennegrass as they went. By the end of the afternoon, they were quite a long way from their tent. As they were hungry, they sat down to eat the food which they had brought with them. The warmth of the sun, which shines day and night in summer in Lappland, and their long walk with all the cutting of the sennegrass, had combined to make them feel sleepy, so after their meal they decided to have a short sleep before returning home. They lay down on the sacks which they had filled with sennegrass—and fell asleep.

When they woke up, they found to their surprise that they were no longer by the river-bank, but inside some kind of cave. And all around them were a number of women in Lapp clothing—none of whom they knew.

Seeing that Ravna and Marish had woken up, these Lapp women came nearer to them, and spoke kindly to them. Ravna was frightened and began to cry, but Marish did not seem to mind being in this strange place, with strange people, and even looked around her in curiosity. Over in one corner she could see a number of beautiful, new Lapp dresses laid out—much finer ones than her own, with wider bands of coloured ribbons along the hem, around the neck, and over the shoulders, than she had ever seen—and all in very lovely colours. Besides the dresses, there were silk kerchiefs of the kind that all Lapp women wear over their shoulders, and also beautiful silver brooches and golden rings and belts hung with silver and gold coins.

All this attracted the elder girl's attention, and when the Lapp women beckoned her over to look at them closer, Marish went to them, and examined the many wonderful things the Lapp women had. When they gave her one of the dresses, a silk kerchief, a belt, with several rings and brooches, she tried them all on—and accepted them all with pleasure, laughing happily.

Ravna was more upset than ever at this, and would not go near the clothes and jewellery, but just stayed where she was, and refused even to look at it all. And all the while she cried, because she wanted to go home.

Then the Lapp women in the cave loaded the table in the middle with all kinds of delicious food, and bade the children come and eat with them. Marish sat down at the table, and ate everything which was offered her, but Ravna wept louder and louder, and would not be persuaded to eat. When the meal was over, the Lapp women talked over what they should do about Ravna, who was now sobbing louder than ever.

'We had better take her back to the place where we found her,' said one of them. 'She is no good to us. But Marish is one of us now, and will stay here.'

The next thing Ravna knew, she was lying on the sacks

of sennegrass again, by the side of Sennegrass River. But she was alone—there was no sign of Marish. Frightened, she left the sacks where they were, and ran home as fast as she could.

Her parents were very surprised to see her come into the tent without Marish, and when Ravna told them of how she and her sister had fallen asleep on the bank of the river, and woken up in a cave where there were a lot of strange Lapp people, her mother said, 'Those must have been "govetter", underworld Lapps, who found you and took you to their underworld cave!'

And her father asked, 'Did they offer you pretty clothes, and jewellery?'

'Yes, they did,' answered Ravna, 'but I did not take them. Marish took all they offered. She tried the clothes on, and kept them.'

'And did they give you food?', asked her father.

'Yes, their whole table was covered with good food. But I did not eat any of it. Only Marish ate of their food.'

'That is why they kept Marish, and let you go,' said her father, 'Once a real Lapp has eaten the food of underworld Lapps, he cannot return to his own world.'

In the night, the children's mother dreamed that a strange Lapp woman came to her and said, 'Do not sorrow for your daughter, Marish. We will treat her well, and she will not want for anything. We live the same life as you do—just in a different world. And when Marish grows up, we will marry her to our richest Lapp youth. We are already fond of this little Lapp girl from your Lapp world—and to show our gratitude for her, we have put something for you under the sacks of sennegrass which your daughters cut, and which are still lying by the river.'

In the morning, the mother went to bring home the sacks of sennegrass, and underneath one of them she found a small pouch with paper money in it. The money was real, and Ravna's parents put most of it by to buy reindeer with, as a dowry for her, when she too grew up and wanted to marry.

15

How to catch underworld animals

THE *underworld* Lapps lived exactly the same kind of life as the Lapps in the *real* world—the only differences being that the former lived below ground, and could make themselves visible or invisible whenever they wanted.

Often, real world Lapps and underworld Lapps lived near each other on the same piece of land, without the real ones knowing that the others were there. Sometimes, both even fished in the same river and lakes—but the underworld Lapps always caught strange fish that no real Lapp had ever been known to catch. The underworld Lapps even had their own herds of reindeer, and migrated with them in spring and autumn, just as the real Lapps did.

Now, any Lapp owner of reindeer always tries to increase the number of his herd in every way he can think of, for the reindeer are the nomadic Lapp's wealth. So the real Lapps were always on the look-out for underworld reindeer which had strayed from their owners, and which they could capture and add to their own herd. These animals were not always visible, any more than their owners were; but if they had strayed off on their own into the mountains, or along the coast, and been away from their underworld owners for more than a week, *then* they became visible— and any real Lapp could see them. However, they would instantly become invisible again if they caught sight of the Lapp before he had captured them—*or* if he took his eyes off them for a single instant before capturing them. Indeed, to catch underworld animals at all, a Lapp had to know exactly *what* to do, and *how* to do it.

One day in summer, two Lapp brothers named Jakko Vars and Arnet Vars came down to Svappavaara from the mountainous country above it. They had been busy with their reindeer all day, and when they got down into the valley they lit a birch-twig fire and sat down beside it to cook a meal and to rest. After their meal, Jakko and Arnet each pulled out a pipe from the folds of his kofta, and smoked in silence, one on each side of the fire, half-lying, half-sitting. All of a sudden, Jakko's attention was caught by something moving, several hundred yards away. His eyes followed the movement—and to his astonishment he soon identified a large reindeer.

'Arnet, I see a reindeer behind that big boulder over there,' he said, pointing in the direction of the movement.

Arnet sat up, and looked in the direction his brother indicated.

'But no one has reindeer in this district except us, and ours are all up in the mountains,' he said doubtingly. 'Besides—I cannot see anything.'

'I tell you I *did* see one—and a big one,' insisted Jakko, 'and I can still see a piece of its antlers, although the rest of it is almost hidden by the boulder.'

'Then it can only be an underworld reindeer!' exclaimed Arnet. 'We can try to catch it—but remember what our father has taught us.'

'I have not forgotten,' Jakko assured him for he had had his eyes fixed intently on what could be seen of the reindeer ever since he had first noticed it.

87

Silently, Arnet and Jakko began to make their way towards the boulder, moving only a few yards at a time, and then stopping. It was more difficult for Jakko to approach the reindeer than for his brother, because, although the animal should on no account see *him*, he had to see *it*, and keep it *constantly* in sight.

The brothers crept nearer and nearer until they were within thirty yards of the reindeer. That was as far as they could get without the animal seeing them for there was nothing further for them to hide behind. The big reindeer came out from behind the boulder, and they could see that it was a magnificent, heavy, fat animal.

'Our father has taught us that the only way to catch an underworld animal is to throw a piece of steel over it—then it cannot become invisible again,' Arnet whispered.

'My knife is steel. If I could throw that over its back, it would be ours,' Jakko whispered back.

But the distance was too great. Thirty yards was too far for Jakko to throw his knife.

Suddenly, he had an idea! Both the brothers had been busy with their reindeer that afternoon, so both still had their long lassos over their shoulders. Quickly, Jakko unfolded his from where it hung, sideways over one shoulder and under the opposite arm, and tied the knife onto the end of the rope. Then he carefully prepared the long lasso in his hand, in such a way that it would not get entangled in itself when he threw it. He did this all by feel, for his eyes were still fixed on the reindeer.

When he was ready, he took careful aim and his lasso whistled swiftly through the air towards the reindeer. The steel knife flew with it—over the back of the animal, and down on the other side. The big reindeer jumped around, and shook its heavy antlers—but it stayed visible in spite of its efforts. And when a second lasso—Arnet's—was thrown over its antlers, it put up no resistance to being captured by the two Lapp brothers.

'What a handsome animal for our herd!' exulted Arnet.

Jakko agreed, but added, 'I hope it is *you* who see the next underworld animal we come across for it is very difficult to keep one's eyes on it and not lose sight of it for even a second!'

Arnet laughed, and said, 'Let us go and thank our father, that he taught us exactly what to do and how to do it!'

The big buck-reindeer frightens Orbun's herd

16

Strange tales of strange reindeer

OUT in the vast, uninhabited parts of Lappland, where only the wild reindeer roam, there are, here and there, one or two isolated huts. Made of peat-turf cut directly out of the soil, they are put together over a bare ground floor, and often stand thus for many years, before falling a prey to the elements. Few and far between, these 'gamme' as they are called, are used only by an occasional hunter, far from home.

One day, many years ago, a small group of Lapp hunters set out together from Skaidi, into the wide, open country which lay beyond it, to look for wild reindeer. They walked and walked for two days, sleeping the first night in the open; by the second night they had reached one of the gamme out in the wilderness. From there they went out to hunt in a different direction each day, returning to the gamme each night to eat and sleep. In this way they hunted for three weeks.

On their last night in the gamme before returning to Skaidi they all felt very pleased with the result of their hunting, as they sat around the open fire, which burned between the fire-stones on the floor, and cooked their food. When they had eaten, they pulled out their pipes and tobacco, and smoked for awhile in companionable silence, tired from their hunting and drowsy from the food and the warmth of the fire.

Janke Reppen was the first to break the silence.

'We have been lucky,' he said, 'for between us we have caught many wild reindeer. But, in the whole three weeks we have been here, none of us has seen any *underworld* reindeer!'

'Why do you say that?' asked one of the others. 'Have you caught underworld reindeer yourself?'

'I have not *caught* any,' replied Janke, 'but I have *seen* many of them—a whole herd, in fact!'

The others looked at him with interest—and asked him to tell them more about it.

'At the time,' he began, 'I was not hunting wild reindeer as now, but was tending my own herd on the spring migration. The snow conditions were very bad that year, and we had been a long time on the way down from the mountains. But we had almost reached the coast, and I decided to give my herd an entire day's rest.

'When night came and the reindeer lay down to sleep, I stayed with them. I lay down, intending to keep watch as usual, all night. But I was so tired from the long, difficult migration, that, before I knew it, I had fallen asleep.

'I was jolted awake by the sudden sound of the whole herd moving off, and very fast! Hurriedly, I jumped up and ran after the reindeer which I saw running away, to drive them back to the resting-place again. I clearly *saw* a large herd of reindeer—I *heard* the beat of their hooves on the ground—*and* the sound of the bells around the necks of the leader-animals. I ran beside them as fast as I could, to try and get ahead of them—but they were running so fast that I could not catch up with the leader-reindeer.

'Then I saw them go in front of a small hill—and I knew that if I went around the *back* of the hill, the distance would be much shorter, and I would get to the other side before the reindeer did—and could then stop them, and turn them back. But, when I reached the other side of the hill—there was no sign of the reindeer. The whole herd had completely vanished!

'When I went back the way they had come, there was no trace of reindeer hoof-prints anywhere on the ground—they had passed without leaving the slightest mark! And when I returned to the resting-place, there were all my animals as before, not one of them had moved. I found them all in exactly the same place as I had left them before lying down to rest!'

Janke finished his tale, and looked around at his listeners.

There was a few moments silence, then one of them, Orbun Forsa, took his pipe from his mouth, and said, 'I too have seen an underworld reindeer, Janke. I have seen only one—but that one was so big, and had such enormous antlers, that I shall never forget it. If you wish, I will tell you about it.'

The others nodded, so Orbun continued, 'It was just before Christmas one year, and I was tending my reindeer, as you were. In the evening, I stopped at the tent of a Lapp friend, where I was to spend the night. Just as we were making food, another Lapp, Guvda-Elias from Enare, arrived with a number of reindeer and sledges. He was on his way to the nearest town to do some shopping for Christmas, and he too was going to spend the night in the same tent.

'After eating, and putting down my reindeer skins for the night, I went out to see if my reindeer herd was all right.

93

When I came to where they were resting, I was very surprised to find them, not lying down, but jumping about, and running around in all directions. I could tell that they must be afraid of something—but what it was I could not see. In the dark it was very difficult to make out very much, and it took me a long time to discover the cause of their fright.

'At last I came across an enormous, grey coloured, buck reindeer in their midst, which did not belong to me. It's antlers were the widest across of any I have ever seen! It seemed to have broken free out of a sledge-harness, for it had the wooden part around its neck, and a beautifully decorated, wide harness over its back. On the rope by which its owner had lead it, hung a thick clump of wood, which banged from side to side at every one of the big animal's movements. The buck reindeer was afraid of this piece of loose wood, which kept banging against it—and tried to throw it off, by jumping up and down in all directions. But in doing so, it was making all my reindeer more frightened and nervy than ever. None of them would go near the big, strange reindeer—and all of them were running about, left and right, to try to keep away from it.'

'At first I thought it must be the sledge-reindeer which belonged to Guvda-Elias from Enare, and that it had broken loose from his sledge. So I tried to catch it with my lasso. But no matter how often, and how perfectly, I threw the lasso, I just could *not* catch that big reindeer. Such a thing has never happened to me before nor since. Then I looked more closely at it—and I suddenly knew that it must be an underworld animal, for such an enormous reindeer I have never seen amongst our herds.

'As I could not catch it, I decided to make it go away.

So I ran towards it, shouting as loudly as I could, and waving my arms in the air. As soon as it saw this, it was very frightened, as I had hoped it would be, and it ran off, away from my own herd of reindeer.

'The next morning, there was enough light from the moon for me to see the marks of where it had passed—and they led straight down to a narrow passage where a small waterfall fell directly into the river. On one side of the river, right by the waterfall, the marks stopped. And there was no single trace on the other side—although I searched and searched.'

The other Lapps inside the gamme moved uneasily as Orbun came to the end of his story. But one of them could not keep quiet for long.

'I have listened with great interest to what you, Janke, and you Orbun, have to tell of your experiences,' he said, 'and I can tell you of one of my own.'

'Tell us, Mikket Bongo,' said the others, 'for we are all interested.'

Mikket leaned back against the peat-turf sides of the gamme, and began.

'Curiously enough, it also happened when I was tending reindeer. But it was at the time of the autumn migration back to the mountains. I and several other Lapps, whose reindeer all grazed in the same district during the summer, had just spent a long time sorting out all the animals into herds, according to the owner's brand-mark. Then each of us set off with his own herd, to return to the winter pasture-grounds by different ways, so that the herds would not get mixed together again.

'One day, when we were about half-way between the coast and the mountains, I was surprised to see a herd of reindeer coming behind my own reindeer. My herd was on the move—but the other herd was moving so fast that I was afraid they would soon overtake my animals, and be mixed up amongst them. Then the long job of lassoing each animal, and separating it according to owner, would have to be done all over again. So I set my dogs to chase the other herd off, and keep them away from my own animals.

'At first they did not react at all to the barking of the three dogs, and when the leader-animals finally came to a standstill, they were so near that I could see they were all unusually large, with very long ears, and big antlers. And I suddenly realised that they might all be underworld reindeer! I remembered what I had heard—that the only way to capture reindeer belonging to underworld Lapps was to keep one's eye constantly on them—and throw any piece of steel over them.

'By this time, my dogs had made the whole herd turn around—and they were now all running swiftly away, back in the direction they had come from. I only had time to throw my steel knife over the very last one of them—and, just as I had done that, I stumbled over a stone and fell. So, of course, I could not keep my eye constantly fixed on the strange reindeer—and, when I picked myself up again, the whole herd had completely vanished! Except for that one reindeer over which I had managed to throw my steel knife! Grazing quietly nearby was this one big animal—and when I looked at its brand-mark, it was a very strange mark which I had never seen before. And no one else could recognise it either.'

When Mikket had finished telling his strange tale, a long, deep silence fell on all the Lapp hunters inside the gamme.

Each of them was thinking over what he had just heard. At last, Janke stirred himself, and reached over to put the coffee-kettle by the fire, and to make a fresh brew. Mikket put some more birch-wood on the fire, to get it to burn better. Janke opened his mouth to ask Orbun to pass him the pouch with coffee in it—but he did not get the words out.

For suddenly, from outside the gamme, and as yet some distance off, there came an unexpected sound. The sound of a large 'raid', or caravan, of many people and reindeer-sledges, driving fast, and towards the gamme. Who could possibly be on their way in such a wild, lonely part, where only hunters came? All those inside the tent asked them-selves the same question. They heard the whole 'raid' of sledges pull up outside the gamme—and they heard voices as the reindeer were unhitched from their harnesses. Then they heard many reindeer shaking themselves, as reindeer do when they have been released from the sledge-harness. And they even heard the sound of people just outside the gamme, as they knocked the light snow off their clothes and shoes.

The hunters expected that now someone would lift up the door-flap of the gamme, and come inside. But no one did. And although they waited—absolutely no one ap-peared!

At last, Janke and Mikket went outside to see what was happening. The moon had now come out, and they could see clearly for a long way around, on all sides. But there were *no* people—*no* reindeer—and *no* sledges to be seen anywhere! They called the other hunters outside. But none of them could see the people and animals they had all heard so near, and so clearly.

At last Orbun thought of looking for traces in the light

layer of new snow—and he found clear traces of reindeer hooves and sledges, as well as footprints. But the people and animals who had made them had completely vanished! The hunters went back inside the gamme—and Janke looked round at their puzzled faces.

'Now you have all seen and heard something similar to the things Orbun, Mikket, and I told you about. Now *you too* have a strange tale to tell—of strange people—and strange reindeer.'

17

Strong-Sirdar of the Skolts

THE Skolt-Lapps of the village of Neiden have always been especially lucky in one thing—salmon fishing. The river that runs through the village is rich in salmon, especially in one particular place called the Waterfall of Neiden. In the old days, the Skolt-Lapps used to catch the salmon by spreading a net right across the river, just by the waterfall. When the salmon swam up the river in spring and jumped over the waterfall, they fell into the net and were caught.

To the Skolt-Lapps living in Neiden, the salmon was one of their greatest delicacies of the year; they ate it fresh from the river, and they smoked it, over special fires which they made in the open air, in order to be able to keep some of it as food reserves for later.

But they were not the only ones to appreciate the delicious flavour of the salmon from their river. Some Russians had heard about the fantastic amount of salmon in the Neiden river—perhaps from Skolt-Lapps from the Russian Lappland village of Notozero, who had been in Neiden and returned to tell of the wonderful salmon-fishing there. And some of these Russians were so envious of the Skolt-Lapps in Neiden that they planned a way to take the use of the Neiden river away from them, and keep all the salmon for themselves.

One spring day, the Skolt-Lapps laid their net as usual across the river, and then went back to their homes. Later, they would return to carry back the salmon which were caught in the net. Amongst them was a Lapp much bigger and stronger than anyone else in the village. His name was Sirdar Vadnim, and he had defeated all the other Skolt-Lapps in friendly wrestling, and many more besides. For this reason he was known all around as 'Strong-Sirdar of the Skolts'.

On that particular day, a large Russian ship was suddenly sighted coming up the Neiden river—and the Skolts could see that there were at least fifty men aboard. They knew that the Russians must be bent on some kind of trouble, and that they were also better armed. So the whole village fled higher up the river.

When the Russians stopped their ship, and came on shore, they found the whole of Neiden deserted. They had intended to kill any Skolts who put up any resistance, and drive the others out of the village, so that they could have the waterfall and all its salmon for themselves. Now, having no need to fight, they went straight to the waterfall, and gloated over the large amount of salmon that they found in the net. For several days, they set the net in the same way, and pulled hundreds of salmon out of the waterfall. Each time, they congratulated themselves more and more on the good idea they had had to steal this salmon-fishing away from the Skolt-Lapps.

But in the meantime, the Skolts who were in hiding further up the river had sent a scout down to Neiden, to find out what the Russians were doing—and he had reported back that they were not plundering the village, but seemed to be interested only in the net and the salmon.

Strong-Sirdar and the other Skolts held a council as to what should be done, and they came to the conclusion that the only hope was to destroy the net. If they could do this, then the salmon would not be caught—and, as it would take a very long time to repair such a large net, and even longer to make a new one, perhaps the Russians would give up, and go away. It would take men of great courage to destroy the net, for the Russians had put guards on both sides of it, and anyone approaching it would certainly be seen, and the Russians would just as certainly try to kill him. Strong-Sirdar was the first one to volunteer; then two others offered to go with him—and that was enough.

That night, the three of them rowed a small boat down the river, as silently as they could. Luck was with them, for they reached the waterfall without mishap. As quickly, and as quietly as possible, they began to pull and tear at the net. It was not easy in the darkness—but they managed to make a number of big holes in it, before the Russian guards saw them.

When a sudden roar of rage told Strong-Sirdar and the two others that they had been discovered, they knew they must escape at once. Quickly, they turned their small boat around, and rowed as fast as they could back towards their hiding-place up-river. But the Russian guards had a much bigger boat—and, with ten of them rowing it, they soon overtook the three Skolt-Lapps. At the very last moment, the three of them managed to reach the river-bank, and jump ashore. Then they ran off, and hid in the darkness.

The ten Russians, thinking that there might be many more Skolt-Lapps hidden, did not follow them onshore, but instead called out, 'We will not kill you tonight! But come tomorrow into Neiden, all of you Skolt-Lapps! If you do not come—we shall come here, in daylight, and kill you all in your hiding-places! And when you come, your Strong-Sirdar, of whom we have heard, shall wrestle against our chief. He is one of the strongest men in the whole of Russia—and he will make any Lapp look as weak as a flea! When our chief has killed him—then we will kill the rest of you!'

With these threats, the Russians rowed away again.

Slowly, the three Skolts returned to the place where the others were hiding. The next day, all the Skolt-Lapp men, and even the youths and the strongest amongst the women, armed themselves with a wooden club cut from a stout branch—and went into Neiden, where they found the Russians waiting for them. Their chief was a big man, who was striding up and down, beating his chest with his fists, and shouting, 'I will show that Skolt-Lapp which of us is the strongest! Then people will no longer call him Strong-Sirdar, but Sirdar the flea!'

When Sirdar appeared over the brow of the hill, at the head of the Skolt-Lapps, the Russian chief stopped his posturing and boasting in sudden surprise that a Lapp could be so big. The Lapps are usually quite small people, and the Russian had not expected to be confronted with such a big adversary. Strong-Sirdar strode towards the Russian chief—and the nearer he came, the bigger and stronger he seemed to get—until the Russian, a big man himself, was suddenly afraid of this Skolt he had to fight.

'I will not kill you!', he said quickly, when Strong-Sirdar was three feet away from him, 'and my men will not kill your people either—if you will agree to let us have all the salmon on the Neiden river—now, and in the years to come. You and your people can have any other fish in the river—but every year, we will come, and take the salmon. That is my condition to let you now go in peace.'

Strong-Sirdar looked round at the rest of the Skolts—and on their faces he could read the same thoughts as were in his own head.

'No,' he answered, 'the river and the salmon are *ours*. We will fight now—you and I—and when I have defeated you, you can have the choice; either I kill you at once, or you and your men leave immediately and never return to Neiden.'

With the eyes of all his men upon him, the Russian chief had to agree to fight. He was one of the best wrestlers of his country, and he had defeated many of his countrymen—but he was no match for Strong-Sirdar. The fight was violent, but short. When he had the Russian chief pinioned helplessly beneath him, Strong-Sirdar asked, 'Now the choice is yours—shall I kill you, and let my people fight your men? Or shall I spare you—on the condition that you all leave, and never set foot in Neiden again?'

The Russian chief chose to be spared and give up all thoughts of taking the rich salmon-fishing away from the Skolts. As the large Russian ship left down the Neiden river, Strong-Sirdar stood on the river-bank, and called out to the Russian chief, 'When you get back to your country, tell any others who may plan to steal the salmon in the Neiden river, that Strong-Sirdar of the Neiden Skolts is a *big* flea—and one who knew how to *bite*!'

Noralda's mother wept over her baby in his cradle

18

Noralda and the invisible people

ALTHOUGH there are many stories about the 'govetter' or underworld people, there are very few about the 'halder', or invisible people. The former could make themselves visible whenever they wanted to, and also often came to the real Lapps in a dream. But the invisible people were never seen at all; in the whole of Lappland there were only a very few people who *knew* they existed, and of those few, only two or three had actually had *proof* of their existence, as a result of extraordinary circumstances.

But everyone knew where the invisible people had *come from*—for there is a very, very ancient explanation of them, which goes all the way back to the time of Adam and Eve. It seems that Adam and Eve had a lot of children, and one day God decided to visit them, and see how they were. Eve wanted her children to look their best, so she called them all in, and started to wash them. But there were so many of them that she did not manage to get them all washed in time, before God arrived. So she hid all the ones who were still dirty.

God looked at the children, and did not see as many of them as he had expected; so he asked Eve if those were all she had. Eve lied, and said they were, and that she had no others. But God, who knew she was deceiving him, said, 'Let those who are hidden from God, stay hidden from the eyes of all peoples. From now on, they and their descendants shall wander the earth and remain invisible!'

So all the Lapps knew that this was how there came to be invisible people in Lappland. Many strange happenings and events were said to have been caused by these totally invisible people—but practically no one could say it was so for sure.

But there was one person who had no doubts at all. This was a little eight year-old Lapp girl called Noralda Turi—and she *knew*. How did she know? All because one day, when she was playing by herself a long way from the tent where she lived with her parents, she found a very strange-shaped little jar, which attracted her attention as it shone in a ray of sunlight. Noralda had never seen a jar like that before, and so she picked it up, and began to play with it, wondering who could have dropped it in a place where no one lived and almost no one passed.

Curious to see if there was anything inside it, she opened the lid, and found it was full of a fragrant whitish cream. It smelt so nice that she rubbed one finger over it, and then held the finger up to her nose, to smell it better. Then she rubbed some on her other hand, and smelt it again. A mosquito (of which there are a tremendous lot in Lappland in summer) was also attracted to the fragrant smell, and it buzzed nearer to smell it better. It flew right into the jar, just as Noralda lifted the jar to her nose to smell it better. As it flew out again, it flew up into Noralda's eye, and she was so afraid that it might sting her eye, that she quickly rubbed it with her finger, to try to get it out. Now, it so happened that that finger was covered with the fragrant cream from the pretty, mysterious jar!

Almost immediately Noralda was surprised to see a strange-looking woman, dressed in a kind of clothing which she had never seen before, moving quickly over the rough ground nearby, poking with a stick amongst the earth and stones, as though she were looking for something. Suddenly, this woman caught sight of Noralda—and of the little jar which she was still holding in her hand. She rushed towards the little Lapp girl, and seized the jar from her hands, then turned to go away again. Noralda began to cry.

'Why did you take the pretty jar away from me?', she asked, 'I found it—and so it is *mine*!'

The strange woman turned around again, and looked at her in astonishment.

'Can you *see* me?' she asked.

'Of course I can see you,' answered Noralda crossly.

'But—if that is true—then you must have rubbed some of this magic cream on your eye! Otherwise, I would be invisible to you,' said the woman slowly.

'You are *not* invisible at all,' said Noralda, 'and I want the jar back that I found! Please—give it back to me!'

'Little girl,' said the strange woman, 'I cannot give you this jar—nor the magic cream which is inside it. But the jar itself has already given you a very valuable gift—the ability to see the invisible people! Perhaps, some day, this gift will be of great use to you!'

Noralda did not believe much of this, and was more interested in getting back the pretty jar and the fragrant cream than anything else. She cried bitterly when the strange woman refused to give it to her—and even more when she suddenly walked away, moving very fast until she was lost in the distance. Still crying, Noralda went back to her parents' tent, and told them what had happened.

Her mother thought she had probably dreamt the whole incident, and, in any case, there was no further way, at the time, of telling whether Noralda really could see the invisible people now, or not.

But two years later, when Noralda was ten years old and had a new baby brother who was only a few months old, a strange thing happened. One summer day, her father was out fishing in his boat on the lake beside which their tent was pitched, and her mother was in the nearby forest, cutting birch-wood twigs and branches for her fire, to do the cooking on. Noralda herself was some distance from the tent, weaving bands of coloured wool for the winter shoes. The other children, all boys, were fishing with their father. And so the three-months-old baby was alone in the tent.

Busy weaving, within sight of the tent, Noralda suddenly saw two strangely-dressed women walk up to the tent, and go inside it. Who could they be? And what did they want, just when the whole family was absent? Noralda laid down her weaving, and decided to go and ask them. At the edge of the forest, she could see her mother returning, carrying wood.

But before Noralda reached the tent, the two strange women came out of it—and one of them was carrying her baby brother! They looked around, then started to hurry off. At Noralda's loud cry of alarm, her mother dropped the wood she was carrying, and ran to see what was the matter.

'Two strange women have stolen the baby!' cried Noralda, pointing in the direction in which they had gone.

Her mother hurried into the tent to see if it was true, and then hurried out again after Noralda, who had already started to chase after the two strange women. The two women carrying the baby in his cradle could not go as fast as the fleet-footed little Lapp girl and, seeing that Noralda was catching up with them, with her mother close behind, they gave up the idea of stealing the baby, and put him down in the middle of the path. Noralda picked him up, and handed him to her mother, who wept at the danger he had been in. Noralda pointed to the two strange women, clearly visible to her, about a hundred yards away.

'There they go,' she said, 'and they both look like the strange woman who took the pretty jar away from me, two years ago.'

Her mother looked—but she could not see anyone, no matter how much she searched the surroundings, near and far, with her strong Lapp eyes, used to distinguishing things over great distances.

'Perhaps it is true, then, that you can see the invisible people,' she said slowly. 'And if that is so, it is a very valuable gift indeed, for it has just enabled you to save your baby brother. And never again will I leave him alone in the tent.'

And, even to this very day, the Lapps still have a saying: 'Never leave a child alone in the tent.' And they are careful to take all their children with them, whether they are fishing, cutting wood, or whatever they are doing.

19

The water-folk of Karasjok

THERE were two different kinds of invisible people, or 'halder' as they were known in Lappland. One kind lived on land and the other kind lived below water, in the rivers and the lakes. Although no one had ever seen them, all the Lapps knew that they were there, for very often, when they were fishing, the water-folk had given them proof of their existence.

Long, long ago, when the first Lapp came to Karasjok, he found that the water-folk were already there before him. This man's name was Abram Joks, and he had fallen on bad times. In his youth he had been a reindeer-owner, but he had always been unlucky, and year after year his herd had diminished, until at last there was only a handful of animals left—and finally he had to sell even those, to raise money for food and clothing, for himself and his family. The only thing for him to do then was to try to live from hunting and fishing.

For the first time in his life, he had a stroke of *good* luck—for he came to a beautiful part of Lappland which was rich in wild animals to hunt in the forests, with fish in the river, and berries in the open country nearby. Today, this place is called Karasjok, but when Abram Joks came to it he was the first Lapp to settle there, and it had no name.

The first thing Abram did was to build himself a 'gamme', or peat-turf house, which he cut directly out of the soil. Next, he went hunting in the forests to provide food for his family, and if he was lucky enough to come across an elk, which is a large animal, then there was plenty of meat for quite a long time. As soon as he could, he dug up the ground around his gamme, and planted potatoes. That was the only thing he had to plant.

When all that was done, he began to think about fishing in the long, winding river (beside which the village of Karasjok now lies). But he had no boat. So this time when he went back into the forest, it was to cut down wood to make himself one. It took him a long time, but at last the boat was finished, and he could row it down the river to fish from it—the very first Lapp ever to fish in the Karasjok river.

At first he caught nothing at all—so he rowed to another place and tried there. After a long while, he caught just one, small fish. Again he started to row further down the river, but he had not gone very far, when suddenly a voice said, 'Fish here!'

In amazement, Abram stopped rowing. Where could the voice have come from? There was no one—absolutely no one—anywhere near, for many miles around, except himself and his family. He decided that he must have dreamt it, and started to row again. But he had not pulled more than once on the oars, when again a voice said, 'Fish *here*!'

Again Abram stopped—and this time he looked up and down the river in all directions, and towards both banks of the river. But there was no one there. He had not really expected that there would be—yet this time he was certain that he *had* heard the voice. Very puzzled, he leaned on his oars, not knowing what to think or do.

'Abram Joks—FISH HERE!' came the voice again, suddenly, and to Abram's intense fright it sounded as though it was coming from below the water. Hearing his own name pronounced by an unknown and invisible voice was too much for Abram, and he seized the oars to row away as fast as possible. But, in his attempt to hurry, he dropped one of the oars into the water—and while he was trying to recover it, the voice came again.

'Do not be afraid, Abram,' it said gently, 'I will not harm you—I only want to help you.'

'W-who are you?' asked Abram, trembling. 'And *where* are you?'

'We are the water-folk who live in the river,' the voice answered, 'and we have watched you since the first day you came here. We have seen you try to make a living for yourself, and provide food for your family. And we are glad that you have come to settle here, for we have been here so long alone. You will never see us, for we are invisible to human eyes. And only *you*, the first settler, will ever hear us speak. If other settlers come after you, they will neither see nor hear us—but they will know we are there, by many signs we shall give them, and things that will happen.'

By now, although Abram had recovered his oar, he made no attempt to row away, for he was no longer frightened.

'And now, Abram,' the voice continued, 'if you fish here at this exact place, you will catch plenty of fish. Come here again tomorrow—and the third fish you catch will be a special gift from the water-folk.'

The voice stopped as suddenly as it had begun—and Abram was once more quite alone. He decided to see whether what the voice had said was true or not. He let down his fishing line—and soon felt a fish on the end of it. By the end of the afternoon, he had caught enough fish to feed his family very well, and some over to dry and keep as food reserve for the winter.

The next day, he went back to the same place, and started to fish again. The first two fish he caught were fine, fat river-fish—but the third one was of a kind he had never seen before. It shone and glittered so much in the sunlight that it almost dazzled him—and when Abram pulled it into his boat, he saw why. *All it's scales were made of silver coins*! Abram could scarcely believe his eyes! He stopped fishing for that day, and rowed back to his gamme, where his wife carefully scaled the fish.

'Perhaps they are not real coins,' she said doubtfully.

But when, some weeks later, Abram went on a journey to the nearest place where he could buy food, the trader accepted his coins after examining them carefully, and Abram was able to bring his family flour, sugar, and all kinds of good things which they had not seen for a long time. They only spent the money on food and other necessities—and in this way the silver coins lasted them for many years.

And every time Abram fished in the place where the voice had spoken to him, he caught plenty of fish, and his family never went hungry.

In time, other Lapps came to Karasjok—built themselves a gamme to live in, and settled there. They found plenty of wild berries—red Arctic-lingonberries, and amber-coloured cloudberries—and plenty of good hunting in the forest; but although they all fished in the river, none of them caught as many fish as Abram did.

Several hundred years later, the Lapps of Karasjok believed, in fact, that the water-folk in the river were there to *protect* the fish, and stop too many of them from being caught. One Lapp in particular, Guttur Eira, was sure that this was so.

He was asleep one night, by the large net which the fisher-Lapps of Karasjok had by that time found out was the best way to catch the salmon which swam up the river in spring. The net was spanned right across the river, from one bank to the other, and was held in position by several long poles. Guttur was watching over the net—but as no one would be likely to interfere with it, he had allowed himself to fall asleep. As no one knew exactly when the salmon would come, the net had already been there some time, and quite a number of salmon were caught in it. Soon there would be more, and the fisher-Lapps would empty it.

Suddenly, Guttur was awakened by an unusual noise. Sleepily, he opened his eyes, without moving from where he lay. To his surprise, he saw that the net had been lifted right out of the water—and the unusual noise was made by the water running out of it onto the surface of the river—*and* by all the salmon, which were now free, jumping and swimming up-river. Thoroughly awake now, Guttur jumped up with a shout—and the very instant that he moved the net fell back into place, and everything was as it had been before. Except, of course, that now most of the salmon had gone. There was no one to be seen—and not a further sound to be heard.

No one in Karasjok blamed Guttur for what had happened, as they knew it was the work of the water-folk. For had not the water-folk said to Abram, 'If other settlers come here, they will never see or hear us—but they will know we are there, by many signs we shall give them, and things that will happen.'

And this was one of the many things they had promised.

'THIS is a nose that's a NOSE!' croaked the Draug

20

Danil learns to defeat a Draug

THE fisher-Lapps who lived by the sea could tell many tales of the strange sea-creature which they called a 'Draug', and which was very different from the friendly water-folk who lived in the rivers and lakes. A Draug lived only in the sea, and was a very nasty-looking creature, with an ugly face and masses of tangled seaweed for hair.

One day, a little fisher-Lapp boy called Danil Tappio, who lived by the sea near Kemi in Finnish Lappland, went with his father, Sarak Tappio, to look for pieces of wood which had been thrown up by the sea onto the shore. Danil was twelve years old, and he often went with his father to help him, whether fishing or collecting the drift-wood that was useful for a number of purposes. But, in all his twelve years, he had never yet seen a Draug. However, on that particular day, and in those that followed, he was to find out all he needed to know on the subject.

Early in the morning, his father took out their boat, and Danil helped him push it into the sea, jumping onto the bows at the last moment. Sarak Tappio rowed and rowed, until they came to a part of the shore where there was always some drift-wood to be found. All that day, Danil and his father collected the wood, and carried or dragged it to where they had anchored their boat. When they had enough wood, they stacked it up carefully in the boat, so that it would not fall out or overbalance them on their way back.

By this time Danil and his father were both tired and hungry, and as there was an old, abandoned peat-turf gamme on that part of the shore, they decided to have a short rest there, and cook the food which they had brought with them, before rowing home. They soon lit a fire, and began to heat water to make a hot soup in the pan they had brought with them.

Danil lay on his right side, on the floor of the gamme, leaning on his right elbow and watching his father fan the flames with his high, Lapp hat. All of a sudden his attention was attracted by a movement at the top of the gamme, by the open smoke-hole. An ugly-looking face was looking down through this hole, and in the middle of the face he could see a huge, flabby nose.

'F-father—look!' cried Danil in great fright, pointing upwards.

Sarak Tappio, surprised at the sound of alarm in his son's voice, looked up, and the owner of the ugly-looking face, seeing that he had attracted their attention, grinned a horrible wide-mouthed grin down at them, from the top of the smoke-hole above their heads. Then he screwed his face up into a series of grimaces, each one more hideous than the one before, and croaked in a harsh voice, 'THIS is a nose that's a NOSE!'

Quickly, Danil's father seized the big ladle which was in the pan of hot water over their fire, and flung a ladleful of boiling hot water upwards at the ugly face. 'And THIS is hot water that's HOT!', he cried.

With a yell of rage, the ugly face disappeared from the

smoke-hole, and Danil and his father heard someone falling off the side of the gamme, and then hurrying away towards the water.

Danil was still too frightened to move, but his father lifted the door-flap of the gamme in time to see a big, ugly Draug crawling back into the sea, and rubbing its nose as it went. He watched until it had disappeared—then turned back to his son, with a look of satisfaction on his face.

'It's a long time since I last saw a Draug,' he said, 'and as for you, Danil, that is the first one you have ever seen. They are afraid of heat—so if you ever see another one, you know now what to do. Throw hot water, or a piece of burning wood at them—and they will go away.'

'But—how did you know what to do father?', asked Danil, 'for I have never heard you tell of meeting a Draug before.'

His father laughed. 'I knew because *my* father told me,' he said, 'and I have never told you about it because I had almost forgotten it, until now. It happened many years ago, when I was a boy not much older than you.'

By now their food was hot, and they both ate in silence. When they had finished, Danil asked his father to tell him more. Sarak Tappio took out his pipe, filled it with tobacco, lit it—then took up his tale.

'I was with your grandfather, *my* father, and several other fisher-Lapps in the big boat which they used for fishing off the coast in the summer. We had been out since very early that morning, and we had fished all day and well into the night, for, being summer, it was as light at night as it was in daytime. Shortly before midnight, my father decided that we had caught enough fish, and we started to row for home. We had not gone very far when

I suddenly saw a small boat coming rapidly towards us. It was strange to see a boat at that hour, for we had not seen another one all day, and indeed there were no other fisher-Lapps living anywhere near. When it came nearer, we could see that there were three people rowing it—but we could not see who they were because they all wore heavy oilskins and sou-westers. This struck me as very odd, because the weather had been calm all day, and at that very moment the Midnight Sun was sparkling on the water, and bathing everything in its soft, golden glow. I saw that my father was watching the boat and its occupants very intently.

'"Stop rowing, and raise all the oars in the air," he ordered.

'I knew that raising the oars in the air was the usual way amongst fisher-Lapps for the fishers in one boat to signal to those in another that they wanted to talk to them. Immediately, the three rowing in the other boat also stopped, and raised their oars in the air, too. The two boats were now quite close to each other. All at once, the three rowers turned to look in our direction, and at last we could see their faces, under their sou-westers. *And we saw that each one of them was no fisher—but a Draug*! Seeing our boat quite alone, they had come to do us some evil.

'But my father was quicker than they were. He reached over to the stove we had onboard, where we cooked our food when we were out fishing for a long time. Luckily it was still hot, for when we had stopped fishing, we had made some hot soup before starting to row for home. He seized a hot, still smouldering piece of wood—and threw it straight at the small boat. It hit the nearest Draug, knocking his sou-wester off, and revealing a head covered with thick, tangled seaweed. And the next instant, the boat disappeared entirely, leaving not a trace on the surface of the sea, to show where it had been. My father turned round to the other fisher-Lapps in his boat, and said, "Now we must row—and row as fast and as hard as we possibly can; for if one ever sees a Draug wearing oilskins and a sou'wester, one can be sure that a storm is going to blow up!"

'We started to row again, each man pulling hard on his oars and, just as we came within sight of where we lived, the Midnight Sun vanished behind sudden clouds, and the wind started to blow. It took all our efforts to row the boat to shore—and when we had at last pulled it up on land, the wind was blowing fiercely, sending the waves higher and higher.

"There will be storm-weather now for three days," said my father, "one day for each Draug we saw." And he was right.

'Since then I have not seen another Draug—until today.'

Sarak Tappio knocked out his pipe on his boot, as he came to the end of his tale. Danil had listened fascinated—and all the way home, as he and his father rowed their own small boat, laden with drift-wood, back to Kemi, he could not forget the ugly Draug he had seen looking down at him from the smoke-hole—nor the tale his father had just told him of the Draug which *he* had seen as a boy.

A few days later, his grandfather, old Olai Tappio, came on a visit to his son's family and, as soon as he could get the old man's attention, Danil told him about his frightening experience of a few days earlier. Sarak Tappio reminded the old man of the time they had seen not one Draug, but three.

Old Olai looked at young Danil, and said thoughtfully, '*I* did not see any Draug until I was a man of thirty—but the one I saw I shall never forget, for he tried to drown me, and I had to fight for my life!'

'Do tell me about it, grandfather,' pleaded Danil—and old Olai was quite happy to tell his son, who had heard it before, and his grandson, the story of his fight with a Draug.

'It was one night when I had been out to see to my fishing lines,' he began. 'There was a certain place, not far from shore, where I used to leave them, and where I could always be fairly sure that when I came back, there would be fish in them. That night, I was returning from putting them out. As I walked back along the shore towards home, I saw the dark shape of something waiting by the water's edge, about a hundred yards away. I could not see what it was, for it was a very black night—but I had the strangest feeling that it was *me* he was waiting for.

'I walked nearer and nearer, for I had to pass along there to reach home, and, with every step, I tried to make out who it was, standing there so still in the darkness. Not until I was absolutely level with it did the dark shape move. Then it suddenly lurched towards me—and I felt a heavy, slimy hand grip my arm and start to pull me towards the water. A Draug—it could only be a Draug! They were known to try any way they could to drown people, especially someone on his own, as I was.

'A second slimy hand joined the first one on my arm—but now I had realised that I must fight for my life, if I were to stop the Draug pulling me into the water, and down to the depths of the sea-bed. I pulled hard in the opposite direction, for I knew that the nearer a Draug was to the water, the stronger it became—and the further onshore I could pull it, the weaker it would become. I pulled and tugged upwards for all I was worth—and at the same time I tried to shout for help. But to my horror I found that I had lost my voice! This sudden discovery frightened me so much that I stopped pulling for a fraction of a second. It was long enough for the Draug to gain the advantage again—and he tugged and pulled so hard that I found myself with my feet in the sea, at the water's edge! Unless I could fight back quickly I would be lost!

'In desperation, I more than redoubled my efforts, and succeeded in pulling myself out of the water onto dry land—then higher up—then, at last, so high up that I was above the high-tide level, the highest point that the sea ever reached. I was quite exhausted by the terrible effort of fighting backwards, uphill, against a heavy, slimy Draug that was doing its best to drag me in the opposite direction. But the moment my feet touched a place on the shore above the high-tide level, the Draug suddenly dropped his grip on my arm and slunk back into the sea. For no Draug has any strength or power against a person who is standing above the high-tide level.

'Very shaken from the fight, I walked home, and when I got there I was careful not to look at any light or fire until the next night. For a person who has fought a Draug has fought such a horrible sea-creature that he must protect his eyes from any kind of light until an entire day has passed. And it was not until the same time that I got my voice back, and could explain to my wife—your grandmother, Danil—what had happened to me.'

Danil's eyes were still fixed on his grandfather, as old Olai finished his story. For a long time the three of them—old Olai, Sarak, and Danil, three generations of a fisher-Lapp family—sat in silence, each one lost in his own thoughts.

But after a while they heard a strange wailing sound

coming from the direction of the sea. It sounded like someone in distress, calling for help. The three of them went outside to hear better—and they could distinctly hear the wailing cry for help from the sea. Old Olai looked down at young Danil, and said, 'It may be *really* someone calling for help. But very often it is only a Draug imitating a human calling—and those who take out a boat to the rescue will be drowned. A Draug will try many ways to lure people to the bottom of the sea.'

'But grandfather—how can one tell if it really is a person who is calling for help, or only a Draug?' asked Danil anxiously.

'The only way is to take a knife, and lay it between your teeth, with the cutting-edge towards the sea,' answered old Olai. 'If it is just a Draug that is calling, then the knife will cut his false wailing, and it will stop at once. But if it is really a human in distress, then the call for help will go on.'

Sarak Tappio had already gone inside to get a knife, and when he came outside again, he laid it between his teeth, with the cutting-edge pointed towards the sea. Immediately, the wailing stopped.

'You see, Danil, it was only a Draug,' said his grandfather.

After that, whenever Danil remembered that there was such a thing as a Draug lurking in the depths of the sea, he was no longer afraid. For between them, his father and grandfather had taught him what to do if ever he came across one. He felt confident of defeating any Draug, thanks to what they had taught him. And one day, as yet far off in the future, he would remember to teach it to his own son.

21

Ghosts from the four corners of Lappland

In the old days, a big market used to be held every Christmas in the village of Enare, in Finnish Lappland. It was one of the big events of the year, and from all over Lappland, Finnish, Swedish, Norwegian and Russian Lapps met there to buy and sell. It also gave them a chance to meet friends and relations whom they otherwise seldom saw during the rest of the year, and to exchange news and gossip, or hear about any interesting or unusual events there might be to tell. And usually there were several Lapps who could tell of new and recent experiences with a *ghost*—for it is in the dark time of winter when there are twenty-four hours of night every day that the ghosts come out in Lappland. In summer, with its twenty-four hours of daylight every day, they hide.

Now, one year when the market was being held as usual, a group of Lapps came together in the evening to talk and enjoy each other's company. The news and events of the past spring, summer and autumn were told and retold amongst all those present, and when they reached the events of the winter, as far as it had gone, a Lapp from the Russian village of Boris-Gleb was the first to start the ball rolling with a new ghost story.

'It was the evening before I left Boris-Gleb to come here,' began Ivvar Jakvitch. 'I was at home in my tent, and my evening meal was cooking in the big cauldron on its chain. All at once, I heard someone driving a reindeer-sledge towards my tent. I thought it was someone coming to visit me, and I was glad that I had put plenty of meat in the cauldron that evening. Nearer and nearer he came—but then to my surprise I heard him drive on *past* my tent, without stopping. I heard his reindeer breathing heavily, and, as he passed my tent, his sledge came so close that it knocked against the door-flap. From the inside of the tent, I saw the door-flap move when the side of the sledge hit it. Then he was gone again—without stopping, or coming inside.

'I could scarcely believe it, so I went outside the tent to see whom it could have been. But I could not see anyone, near or far, and in the snow there were no traces of either the reindeer or the sledge, although fresh snow had just fallen. When I looked at the door-flap, I saw that the piece of wood that fastened it was broken. The driver of the mysterious sledge had broken it, when he knocked against it as he drove past! Then I remembered that this was the dark winter month of December, when the ghosts are restless and very active. And I knew that the mysterious sledge and reindeer, which had so totally vanished, must have been driven by a ghost-Lapp.

'I asked an old village woman what the meaning could be of the visit to Boris-Gleb of this ghost-Lapp and his reindeer. She told me that such a visit could only mean that the custom of keeping reindeer would sooner or later die out in Boris-Gleb.'

As Ivvar Jakvitch came to the end of his story, his hearers

sighed and groaned at the thought of a Lapp village without reindeer, around which the lives of all nomadic Lapps are built. But it had reminded Bure Gaino from Kautokeino in Norwegian Lappland, about an experience that *he* had just had.

'Something strange happened to me on my very journey here,' he said, and everyone turned in his direction. 'I had left Kautokeino early, and driven my reindeer and sledge all day—and by evening I came to the place where Norway and Finland meet. I passed the border, and then from the top of a high hill I could see down onto a small, flat piece of land which lay in front of the hill, and over to a large frozen lake which lay beyond. It was a clear moonlit night, and on the lake, coming towards me, I could see a long raid of at least twenty reindeer and sledges. In the stillness I could hear the bell of the leader-reindeer. I watched for awhile, as the raid came nearer. Then I drove my own reindeer and sledge down the back of the hill, where it was less steep, and round onto the flat ground below. In so doing, I of course lost sight of the raid.

'I thought that when I reached the lake I would be able to see them again—and I would stop for a rest and a chat with whoever was journeying with the raid. But, when I got to the lake—there was no sign of anyone at all! No reindeer—no sledges—nothing! And there were no traces at all of the raid in the snow on the lake. Absolutely everything had completely vanished!

'Then, just as you did, Ivvar Jakvitch, I remembered that this was the month of December, and that it must have been a ghost raid that I had seen. If only I had known *that* when I was still on top of the hill, then I would have stayed where I was, and not lost them out of my sight for an instant. And I keep wondering whether, *if* I had done that, I would have seen where they went—or not.'

Again a sigh went over those who had listened—and it was some time before anyone spoke. At last Paavi Aikio, a Finnish Lapp from Enare itself, broke the silence.

'My story is not quite so recent as yours,' he said, looking first at Ivvar Jakvitch, then at Bure Gaino. 'For it happened to me at the end of last winter. I was fishing through a hole in the ice, on the lake near here. I did not catch many fish that day, and when I at last stopped fishing and started on my way home, my sledge was as light as though it were empty. The snow was heavy and slushy in many places, so I helped my reindeer by walking ahead of him, and pulling him by the rope.

'Being discouraged by the result of the day's fishing, I began to talk to myself, to try and cheer myself up, but I soon got tired of using real words that there was no one else there to hear, and I began to mutter a jumble of sounds, which came out something like this, "Taren, taren—skel, skel! Taren, taren—skel, skel!" While I was muttering this, I heard someone come running behind me, and the sledge suddenly became so heavy that it was almost impossible for me to pull it! I looked round but everything looked just the same as before. There was no one on it. Yet still I had to pull and tug and strain at my sledge, to make it move forward at all. I could not understand it. I turned the sledge upside down, knocked it hard, and turned it the right way up again. But when I tried to pull it, it was still as heavy as before! Then I slowly began to realise that there must be a winter ghost in it.

'For a while I did not know what to do. At last I remembered what I had heard old folk say was the best way to get rid of any ghost that came out of nowhere, and was troublesome. I walked all around the sledge, making the sign of the Cross as I went. Then I pulled on the rope again. And this time the sledge was as light and easy to pull as it had been to begin with.

'That taught me that one should be very careful what one says when one is all alone out in the wide, open country. For if one mutters rubbish to oneself, as I did, it might bring a ghost to trouble and annoy one.'

Paavi Aikio looked round warningly, as he finished his story.

The last one to tell a ghost story that day was Jowna Bals, a Lapp from near Vittangi, in Swedish Lappland.

'Just over a month ago, in November,' he began, 'a group of Lapps came with their reindeer and tents to a place about twenty miles from Vittangi. They stayed there for some time—then the menfolk took the reindeer to a place on the other side of Junosuando. They left the womenfolk behind in three tents and, when they came through the village of Vittangi, they asked me if I would take bread out to the womenfolk. The next day I set out, with a large quantity of bread, for the place where the three families and three tents were. I knew there were three tents, because the menfolk had said so.

'I covered the twenty miles on my skis, but when I came within sight of the tents where I had been told they would be, to my surprise I saw that there were *four* tents, not three. I could see smoke rising out of the smoke-hole on all four of them, but it seemed to me that the smoke coming out of one of them was much thinner than that coming out of the other three. When I came near to the tents, I could see even better that there really were *four* of them.

'I went inside one of the tents, and gave the womenfolk the bread I had brought for them. They were all together in this tent, preparing a meal. They at once offered me food and, while I was eating, I said, "I thought there were only three families here."

'One of the womenfolk answered, "Yes, that is right. We are three families who are related to each other, and we always travel together with all our reindeer."

' "But, when I came, I saw *four* tents," I said, puzzled.

' "Oh no," they laughed, "the menfolk have taken the fourth tent with them."

'I did not say any more, as I did not want to frighten them. But when I left to return to Vittangi, I looked again, very carefully, to see if there were still *four* tents. But now— there were only *three*! The fourth one, to which I had passed so close on my way in that I could have reached out and touched it, had completely vanished! And, although I looked back several more times, it did not reappear. Then I knew it could only have been a tent belonging to a ghost-Lapp.'

Jowna Bals came to the end of his story, then added, 'In Lappland, *many* strange things happen, which we cannot understand, or explain.'

Ivvar Jakvitch, Bure Gaino, and Paavi Aikio looked at him and nodded their heads. They knew this was true, from the strange inexplicable things which had happened to all of them. And the rest of those present left Enare with four new stories of ghosts to tell and think about, during the long, dark winter. Four stories which came from four quite different parts of Lappland. And as he left, each one of them half hoped, half dreaded, that, by the next Christmas market in Enare, *he too* might, perhaps, have a ghost story to tell.

22

Christmas traditions and Ghosts

IT is during the two weeks from just before Christmas until just after the New Year that the ghosts are most particularly active in Lappland. Then it is, that *all* of them come out from the places they have been hiding in during the rest of the year. Even the children know this—and so, during that time, they keep very close to their parents' tent. They put their skis away, for if they were to ski during Christmas and New Year, a ghost would almost certainly come and trouble them. So they stop at home, and help their parents with the preparations for Christmas, for there is a lot to be done.

Firstly, a big pile of wood has to be cut and sawn— enough to last for all the cooking and heating until past the New Year, so that no member of the family will be forced to cut more until then. Secondly, all this wood must be stacked up *neatly and tidily*, although at other times this is not necessary. Thirdly, any small twigs or other pieces of wood which lie on the ground between the tent and where the wood was cut must be swept away, and the whole area left tidy. Special attention must also be given to removing any growing branch, or protruding tree trunk, because on Christmas Night both ghosts and Stallos are abroad, with their own reindeer and sledges, driving from tent-place to tent-place—and if one of their sledges chanced to catch on a tree trunk or branch, near a tent, this would mean instant trouble for the family. For the ghost or Stallo would immediately call for the youngest child in the tent to come out and clear away the piece of wood on which his sledge had caught—and then he might very well carry the child off! And fourthly, outside every tent a pail of water and a plate of meat has to be left, so that any ghost or Stallo who comes by the tent on Christmas Night will find food and drink outside, and will not need to come inside the tent to search for them.

These are customs which are the same all over Lappland.

But there are some Lapp villages which seem to be more prone to ghosts than others. And one of these was the Skolt-Lapp village of Pasvik. Year after year, there were so many stories of ghosts appearing there that the inhabitants almost lost count of them all. But *one* person there remembered every ghost story that she had ever heard, and she used her good memory and the stories for a practical purpose.

This was a poor old woman named Sunna-Brita, who had been left a widow with no children to support her. Somehow or other she managed to scrape together a living, mostly by hiring herself out to other people, to sew clothes from reindeer skins in winter and to help gather sennegrass in summer. In autumn she was able to pick cloudberries, Arctic lingonberries, and blueberries, which she then sold. During the Christmas week she went around from one Skolt-Lapp family to another and begged them for reindeer meat, reindeer milk and cheese, dried fish, or whatever they could give her out of their stabbur. In exchange, she always told them one of the many ghost stories which she so carefully remembered. She had been doing this for so many years that, to the Skolts of Pasvik, a visit from old Sunna-Brita, with a new story to tell, had become part of their Christmas tradition.

Some families were generous, and gave her plenty to take away with her. Others gave her much less. One family which Sunna-Brita knew would always receive her well was the Beronka family. So she always kept some of her very best stories for them.

Usually it was of things that had happened to other people that she told. Such as the time that Old Man Biggi was walking back into the village one evening, when all of a sudden he saw *three* ghosts coming towards him! He was so scared that he lay down right where he was and held on to the nearest tree, so that they should not carry him off. He felt the ghosts pulling and tugging at his feet, but he held on to the tree as hard as he could, and after a while they gave up and went away. But when he tried to stand up, he found that somehow he was powerless to move! He lay like this for some time, quite unable to move a muscle. At last a friend of his came along the same way, and said in astonishment, 'What are you doing there in the middle of the road? Get up, and let us go home together!'

'I cannot get up,' answered Old Man Biggi. 'Three ghosts touched me, and they have taken away my power of movement. You must go to the village and get a handcart, bring it back here, put me on it, and wheel me home!'

His friend was very perturbed at this, and asked, 'Is it really so bad that you cannot stand up and walk?'

'Yes, it is,' gasped Old Man Biggi. 'I tell you I cannot move at all! Go *quickly* to the village, get the hand-cart, and come back *quickly*.'

His friend hurried off and soon returned with his brother and a hand-cart. Between them they lifted the still motionless Old Man Biggi onto the hand-cart, and wheeled him back to the village. But they had to lift him off again, and even carry him into his gamme. And it was not until he was inside his own home again that Old Man Biggi recovered the power of movement, which the three ghosts had taken away from him when they touched his feet. This was a story which the Beronka family especially remembered, for they knew Old Man Biggi well.

But one year, Sunna-Brita told them a story of something which had happened to *herself*—and the very interesting thing about it was that it had happened *immediately after she had left the Beronka family's tent, the previous Christmas*! It had been evening when she left, and started towards the place where she had left her boat. When she got there, she saw a strange-looking cow standing beside it, and in the dim light shed by a cloud-obscured moon, it looked to her as though this cow was a dark red colour, and quite unlike any other cow she had ever seen.

Just as she was looking at it uneasily, she heard a voice say, 'Ha! ha! *Go! go!* Ha! ha! *Don't go! don't go!* Ha! ha!', and it seemed to her that this weird voice and weird words came from the strange red cow. In the darkness, and all alone as she was, this frightened poor old Sunna-Brita completely out of her wits, and she took to her heels as fast as she possibly could, clutching the sack with the provisions which the Beronka family had given her. She just ran—and ran—and ran—and later on she could not remember where she had been, nor how she got to the place where she was found in the morning! For, when the next morning came, a group of Skolt-Lapps found her, to their great surprise, sitting on the ice on the river near their tents over twenty miles from where she first saw the red cow! She was still clutching the sack with the provisions—but she could never explain how she got there.

And if the Skolts had not found her when they did, that would have been the end of Sunna-Brita and her ghost stories at Christmas. As it was, this gave her one more story to tell, and one that particularly interested the generous Beronka family, for they felt that it concerned them too.

But one year when she came to them, they had a story to tell of their own, and for once it was her turn to listen to them. The father, Biennu Beronka, told her that he had been on his way back from the Christmas market in Enare, when he made a stop, still some ten miles from the village of Pasvik, for a rest and a meal.

'I knew, as every Lapp knows,' he said gravely, 'that it is dangerous to sleep out in the snow without any covering, in case a snowstorm comes on. But I was so terribly tired that day, and so very sleepy, that I decided to have a short nap before proceeding, as it did not look like snowing. But, tired as I was, I fell into a really deep sleep. And, as it so often does in Lappland, the weather changed very suddenly and brought on a heavy snowstorm.

'There is no doubt at all in my mind that I would have frozen to death then and there if, all of a sudden, a heavy hand had not shaken me by the shoulders, and a voice said, "Wake up—*wake up*, Biennu Beronka—or you will surely freeze to death where you are!" This woke me up in time to see the gravity of the situation I would have been in. There was no sign of any human-being near, although I looked around in every direction. And as I covered the last ten miles into Pasvik, I knew that it must have been a ghost that saved my life!'

Sunna-Brita had listened carefully as he spoke. When he had finished, she said thoughtfully, 'A ghost almost *caused me* to freeze to death—whereas another ghost *saved you* from freezing to death! Perhaps it is the same amongst ghosts as it is among us Lapps—there are some that are bad, and some that are good!'

'I have brought you this little fish,' said the giant

23

The giant and the whale

THERE were never very many giants in Lappland—and those that there were lived and dressed in the same way as the Lapps themselves. The difference between them was, of course, that the giants were much, much bigger, and very much stronger. There was one other difference too: the giants were afraid of the sun. For if ever a ray of sunlight were to touch them, they would instantly be turned to stone. So for this reason, the giants never came out of their huge caves in the mountains when the sun was out, but waited until it went down. And best of all they liked a cloudy, rainy, or foggy day, with no sun at all. Then they could come out in the daytime.

Most of the Lappland giants liked to eat fish, and they fished from their big boats, mostly at night, when there was no sun. The oars of their boats were made of iron, not wood, and with these oars the giants rowed themselves out to sea to fish, far from land and the huge caves where they lived. But they always had to row back before the sun came out. And because they could not enjoy or benefit from the sun, they were very jealous of the Lapps who could, and who did not have to be afraid that it would turn them to stone. And being so jealous of the Lapps, they did whatever they could to harm them.

If a big rock came hurtling down from the mountains and knocked their tents over, the Lapps knew that it was a giant who had thrown the rock. And if a stream where they went to get water suddenly dried up, they knew it was because a giant had drunk it dry. It was practically unknown for a giant ever to do a Lapp family a *good* turn, but there is just one story of such a thing happening to a Lapp family who lived by the sea near Senja.

One night, a giant who lived in a cave nearby was out fishing. He did not catch very much—at least not for him, for a giant has a huge appetite, and needs a vast quantity of food. Absorbed as he was in trying to catch more, he forgot about the time—until he suddenly realised that it was more than time for him to be on his way back to his dark cave, for the sun would soon be up. Frantically, he rowed back towards land, but the wind was blowing against him, and even with his powerful iron oars and his great strength, he knew he would not be able to get back to his cave in time. So he rowed instead towards the nearest piece of land, and when he reached it, he looked around for any hole in the ground, or any old hut or gamme, where he could take cover. But there was nothing at all there except a Lapp tent.

The sun was almost up over the horizon by now, so in desperation the giant ran to the tent, and dashed inside. It was a very large tent, but even so it was as much as he could do to get inside it. The Lapp family who owned it, and who were still asleep there, woke up in great alarm at finding their tent suddenly almost falling down over their heads, and the ground beneath them trembling. And when they realised that there was a giant actually *inside* their tent, and right on top of them, they were more frightened than they had ever been before in their lives!

Seeing their fear, the giant said as soothingly as he could, 'Please do not be afraid! I promise that I will not hurt you. The sun is out, and if I go outside your tent I shall be turned to stone. If you will let me stay inside here until the sun goes down again, I promise you I will reward you well.'

The still frightened Lapp family said he could stay in their tent—not so much because of the reward which he promised them, but because they simply did not know how to get rid of him. They fed him as best they could when they had their own meals—but they were very glad indeed when the sun at last went down (it was early autumn), and they could get rid of their most unwelcome guest.

Several days went by. Then, very early one morning, long before the sun came up, they were once again awakened by the same giant. But this time he was outside of the tent, and he called to them all to come out and see what he had brought them. They stepped outside the tent and the giant said, 'I am grateful that you hid and fed me—and I promised you that I would reward you well. I know that you do not have much food so I have brought you this little fish. Look!'

They all looked—and the 'little fish' which he had brought them proved to be a *whale*! Giants very often caught whales, which made a real meal for them, and the Lapps, too, were very fond of whalemeat, but they did not get it very often. So the Lapp family was very pleased with the 'little fish' which the giant had brought them, and thanked him very much.

Now this family had a cat, and the cat, attracted by the fishy smell of the whale, came out of the tent to see where it came from. But the giant was terrified of cats, and when he saw it, he took to his heels so fast that the earth shook wherever he passed. And it was quite a long time before a giant was heard of again around Senja.

But about five years later, there began to be stories of a giant who was being particularly troublesome towards the Lapps living there. He had thrown a big stone down at their church, and had stolen any amount of their reindeer, to take home to his cave and roast. The Lapps from Senja decided that they would have to get rid of this giant, for goodness knows what else he might do to them if they did not. But it was not so easy to find a way, for the giant was so huge and powerful and in comparison they were so small and weak. Finally one of them remembered the time that a giant hid in one of their tents, and that they had then found out two previously unknown facts about giants— that they were afraid of cats and that they would be turned to stone if ever they went out in the sun.

So three of them, who each owned a cat, took their cats with them one bright, sunny day, and went up into the hills where the giant lived in a huge cave. The ground was littered with bones from all the reindeer the giant had stolen, and when they reached the cave he was sleeping off his last reindeer feast, and snoring loudly. The Lapps released the three cats into the cave, and all three of them went up to the sleeping giant, and scratched his face. In great fright he woke up, and seeing no less than three cats inside the cave with him, in his terror he jumped up and ran as fast as he could away from them. Heedless of everything else, he ran right out of the cave—forgetting the sun! And when the sunlight touched him, it turned him instantly to stone—as the Lapps had known it would! And that was the last of any giant troubling the Lapps of Senja.

But the huge stone is still there, in exactly the same spot.

And anyone who looks at it long enough, will see how very much like a giant in flight it appears. But don't look for the three cats—for you won't find them!

24

Lawrokesh outwits the Karelians

THE boundaries of Lappland have never been clearly defined, and different nomadic Lapp tribes have wandered freely with their herds of migrating reindeer over vast tracts of northern Norway, Sweden, Finland, and Russia. They went where the animals could find their food—a special kind of lichen which does not grow everywhere. In many parts of the Far North, the Lapps were the only humans for hundreds of miles. In other parts there were some Scandinavian settlers, but the Lapps were afraid of them, and stayed mostly amongst their own people. And in certain regions there were other wanderers whom the Lapps soon came to know as real enemies: the roving bands of fierce Tchuders and Karelians.

The Tchuders came from Russia, and were greatly feared by the Russian Lapps who lived on the Kola peninsular. The Karelians came from a stretch of land between Finland and Russia, and the nearest people for them to attack, rob, and kill were the Finnish Lapps who lived near Enare.

The lake of Enare is very big, the biggest in fact in the whole of Lappland, and full of fish, so naturally the Lapps who lived there were fisher-Lapps, with fixed dwellings. Many nomadic Lapps also passed through the region around

Enare, on the spring and autumn migrations with their reindeer herds. Both the fisher-Lapps and the nomads knew that they could never defeat their enemy in open combat, for the Karelians were much bigger and stronger, as well as better armed. Very often, too, there were only a few Lapp families living near each other, and the Karelians usually attacked them in big groups. Long experience of being both weaker and outnumbered had taught the Lapps that the only way to survive attack by the enemy was by *outwitting* them, instead of trying to fight them.

There are many tales of Lapps who, single-handed, defeated a large group of marauding Tchuders or Karelians— just by using their wits and their close knowledge of that part of Lappland in which they lived. Perhaps one of the best known is the story of Lawrokesh, a peaceful man who became a hero to his people, and well known all over Lappland.

Lawrokesh was a fisher-Lapp who lived with his family in a peat-turf gamme by the lake of Enare. In summer he rowed out in different directions on the lake, and fished all day from his boat. In winter, when the whole lake was frozen over, he had to hack holes in the ice and fish through these. But he seemed to know just where the fish were, and even in winter his family never went hungry.

Now one day, his wife decided to visit her sister who lived in nearby Ivalo. She look their children with her. It was some time since she had seen her sister's family, so it was only fitting that she should take them a gift to mark her visit. And what better gift than a piece of reindeer meat? The fisher-Lapps ate plenty of fish from the lake, but they did not often eat meat, as they owned no reindeer. Sometimes they exchanged some of their own dried fish for reindeer meat from one of the nomadic Lapps who passed that way, and this was then carefully hung up in their stabbur, and only used occasionally. Lawrokesh gave his wife a piece to take with her, and took a small piece for himself at the same time.

It was summer, and the sun warmed his back as he worked on a minor repair to his boat, before setting out on the day's fishing. As Lawrokesh worked in the peaceful silence, he thought of the good reindeer meat which he would eat before he left, and of how he would enjoy every bite. He was in no hurry, for the summer nights are as bright as the days in Lappland, and many a fisherman has made his best catch by the light of the Midnight Sun. When he had finished the repair, he left his boat where it was at the edge of the lake, and went into the gamme to cook his meal.

He soon had a fire going between the fire-stones on the floor, and put his meat in a small pot over it. When it was almost ready, he took a special pouch which held reindeer fat and carefully added a lump of this to the pot. In silent anticipation he watched the fat melt and form a thin layer over the top of the reindeer meat and the broth it was cooking in. So shiny was this layer that he could see his face in it.

When the whole family were together and had reindeer meat, it was cooked in the big cauldron, and after the reindeer fat had been added, his children took turns at seeing their reflection in the shiny layer. This always amused them very much, and they spoke of it for weeks afterwards. Smiling to himself as he thought of this, Lawrokesh turned to reach for his food-bowl and eating utensils, which hung in their usual place on the inside wall of the gamme. He had carved them himself out of wood and reindeer horn, as well as those for his family—and each person's eating things were always hung in a set place on the wall.

But when he turned back to the tempting pot of hot reindeer meat, his smile vanished abruptly. For in the shiny layer of fat a face was reflected—but it was not *his* face! Lawrokesh kept perfectly still, partly from shock, and partly because a Lapp's every instinct tells him to keep motionless at the first sign of danger, for fear of making a false move. He was kneeling in front of the cooking pot, sitting back on his heels, and he kept his eyes fixed on the face reflected so clearly in the liquid, shiny fat. Someone must have climbed up the outside of the peat-turf wall and was now looking down inside, through the smoke-hole at the top. It could not be another Lapp, for no Lapp would behave in this way. He would know that he would always be welcome in a fellow-Lapp's gamme, and would come straight in through the low, loose-hanging door. So it was no friend up there! In which case it must be an enemy— and an enemy could only mean one of the dreaded, armed, and murderous Karelians.

The face moved slightly and at the same time there was a sound of hard metal touching some other hard surface. It was muffled by the peat-turf, but loud enough to tell Lawrokesh that the intruder was, indeed, armed. So it *was* a Karelian—and where there was one of these wandering marauders there would be many more, for they always attacked in groups. Lawrokesh was unarmed. He had a bow and arrow true enough, but it was no good at all inside the gamme, for there was not enough room to use it.

The face disappeared. Lawrokesh picked up a long piece

of burning wood from under the cooking pot. It was the only thing he had to defend himself with. Tensely, he waited for attack. But it did not come. Instead he heard a voice shout out, 'You—Lapp who live alone by this lake—we need a guide, to lead us over this big lake to a place where people live. We will do you no harm if you will help us to land there silently.'

Now Lawrokesh knew that the people to whom the Karelian referred were a large group of his own people, fisher-Lapps like himself, who lived on the opposite side of the lake. He knew too that the Karelians always lied when they said they would not harm anybody. In the end, they would rob and murder him too, just as they did others. But for the moment he had no choice. He *had* to pretend to agree to the Karelian's suggestion. Slowly, he put the burning firewood down again.

But already, as he stood up and pushed the loose door open, a plan was starting to form in his mind. Outside, he could see but one Karelian.

'You are alone. Where are the others you spoke of?' he asked.

'There are three boatfulls of them, a little further down the lake,' replied the Karelian threateningly. 'We need a guide, as I said, and when we saw the smoke coming from your gamme, we knew that there we would find one. You live alone, but if you had a family, we would have taken them as hostages, to make sure you guide us aright.'

Hearing this, Lawrokesh was thankful that his wife and children had chosen just that day to go to Ivalo. 'Well, I will guide you,' he said, pretending to be willing. 'Take me to where the others are.'

The Karelian led the way, and soon they came to a place

where there were indeed three boatfulls of men, all impatiently waiting to start for the other side of the lake. The leader looked at Lawrokesh, and said, 'We must set out at once. My men are impatient, for we have not much food with us, and they are hungry. You will sit in my boat, and if you guide us wrongly I will deal with you myself!'

Now Lawrokesh knew that in the middle of the huge, wide lake, was a small island, He had passed it many times in his fishing boat, and his wife and children picked many baskets of tasty cloudberries there every summer. He began to guide the boats in the direction of this island. It took them some time to reach it, for it was way out, very far from all the banks of the lake.

As the Karelians rowed past the island in their three boats, Lawrokesh turned to their leader, and said, 'You told me that your men are hungry. On that island they could find food, for there the cloudberries grow thicker than anywhere else, and there is no one to pick them.'

Now cloudberries have always been (and still are) one of the greatest delicacies in Lappland, and all the Karelians agreed to delay their attack on the people on the other side of the lake, if by doing so they could eat their fill of the luscious amber-yellow cloudberries. They all landed on the island. Lawrokesh pointed to a nearby hillock.

'The best cloudberries grow on the other side of that,' he told them.

Stumbling over themselves in their hurry, all the Karelians made off in the direction he had indicated, leaving one man behind to tie the boats together and guard Lawrokesh. Lawrokesh helped this man as fast as he could, and when they had almost finished tying the boats, he said to him, 'You must be hungry too, but your companions will eat all the cloudberries and leave you nothing unless you hurry after them. Run as fast as you can while there are still some left. In a moment I will follow you myself, when I have just finished tying this last boat.' The Karelian guard, who was both hungry and greedy, thought this was a good idea, and set off at full speed after the others.

Lawrokesh watched until he disappeared behind the hillock. Then he loosened the moorings of the first boat, jumped in and started to row away from the island. The other two boats, still attached, followed it, but the three together were so heavy that Lawrokesh had to row as he had never rowed before, putting all his strength into every stroke of the oars. When he was about two hundred yards from the island, the Karelians came back over the hillock, and roared with rage to see how their boats had gone.

First they went for the guard, whose fault it was, and killed him. Then they started to call across the lake, 'Lawrokesh, Lawrokesh, come back! come back! We will give you silver spoons to eat from if you come back and get us!'

But Lawrokesh just rowed the harder away from the island, and kept rowing until he had brought the boats over to where he lived. Hastily, he tied them up. He then ran up to his gamme and took his bow and all his arrows. These he loaded into his own, small boat. Again he ran up to the gamme, and seized his pot of reindeer meat, which was cold, and a big lump of bread. Then he started to row off again—back in the direction of the island!

About two hundred yards away from it he stopped— and for four days and nights he kept his little boat there. Every time one of the Karelians jumped into the lake, on any side of the island, Lawrokesh heard him, and waited until he was near enough for one of his arrows to reach him. He never missed—and so each time another Karelian sank! From time to time he ate a small piece of meat and some bread—and often just the sight of this tempted another Karalian into the water.

After three days and nights, Lawrokesh had no more arrows left but he stayed there for another day and night, using his oars to hit the Karalians on the head with, when they were near enough. Again, he did not miss. By the fifth day, the Karelians had stopped trying to swim over. Lawrokesh knew they were now too weak to reach the far-off shore anyway, so he rowed back to his gamme.

He found his family and many other Lapps who were all very agitated at the sight of the three Karelian boats, and puzzled by the fact that, whilst the boats had been there for some days, there was no sign of any Karelians. Lawrokesh explained what had happened, and at first they would not believe him. Then some of them rowed towards the island, and saw that everything he had said was true. They decided that the best thing to do was just to leave the rest of the Karelians on the island, until they starved.

When the Lapp families on the other side of the lake heard how Lawrokesh, single-handed, had saved them from certain extinction just by using his wits, they spread the story of his courage far and wide, and never tired of retelling it to their children and grandchildren.

And to his own children, Lawrokesh warned, 'When you see a face in the melted reindeer fat, always make sure *whose* face it is!'

25

A Visit from Iron-Nose

THE Tornio river has Swedish Lappland on one bank and
Finnish Lappland on the other, all the way until it flows into
the Bothnian Sea. Just at the spot where the river meets the
sea is a place with a beautiful Lapp name—Haparanda.

Lapps from nearby regions of Swedish and Finnish
Lappland have always come to Haparanda when there was
something they wanted to sell or buy, for they knew they
could always find people there who had what they wanted
or wanted what they had. And they put on their best clothes
when they went to Haparanda: the heavily decorated tunics
worn by men and women alike, the equally decorated
reindeer-skin coats, and their fine caps.

Each Lapp tribe had (and still has) a different costume, so
it has always been easy to tell which part of Lappland any
Lapp comes from, just by his clothes and his cap. To the
Lapp womenfolk falls the task of making all these clothes—
for themselves, their menfolk, and their children. And
although it takes them many hours of work, they are
extremely proud of the beautiful results they achieve, and
try to outdo each other in both quantity and quality of
decoration.

Now many, many years ago, there lived in Haparanda a
Lapp woman who was well-known far and wide for the

beautifully embroidered collars and belts which she made. They were something very special—because the thread she used was not ordinary thread but *metal* thread. The woman's name was Alet Sirma, and the thread she used was a special tin thread which she made herself. First she melted a thick piece of tin, with some lead, in a pot. Then she poured this through a hollow birch-twig, hollow because she had already removed the marrow inside it. When the tin had set, she cut the twig off, and had then a thickish piece of thread—too thick, however, to embroider with. So she had to make it thinner and more pliable. This she did by forcing it through a series of small holes cut out of a piece of reindeer horn, and when it had been through the last one, which was very narrow indeed, then the thread was very thin, and perfect for embroidery.

Other Lapp women in Haparanda, and other places, made their own tin thread in the same way, but they did not seem to achieve such fine results with it afterwards. For it was always Alet Sirma who did the most beautiful embroidery on belts, collars, and caps, and everyone who saw them talked about them for a long time afterwards.

Now, one day in late autumn, Alet was very busy indeed with her sewing. The first snow had already fallen lightly—and even the second. But still she had not quite finished making the new winter coats of reindeer-skin for the whole family. She had had to help her husband more than usual with the reindeer that autumn, because his brother, who usually helped them, had been ill. This had taken a lot of her time. Then too, every single person in her family seemed to need a new winter coat that year—the coats from the year before were all so worn that they were not really warm any longer. During the last few weeks, Alet had cut and sewn whenever she could, and now the coats were nearly all finished.

That morning, her husband had set off for nearby Tornio, on the other side of the river, taking the children with him. They would be gone for two-three days, and as Alet stood by the tent and watched them all set off, she was glad that each and every one had a heavy reindeer-skin coat, as well as reindeer-skin trousers and shoes, to keep them warm. But there was still one coat unfinished—her own. Indeed, she had barely started on it.

All that day, Alet sewed her coat, but it was not like sewing thin material, because the fur was so thick that each single stitch took time. Her progress was slow. Every now and then she stopped for a short rest, but the sight of the snow around the tent soon sent her back to the sewing of the heavy coat. Late at night she was still sewing—but she was very tired.

Then, just after midnight, she heard a sudden sound outside. This surprised her very much, because no one else lived near her tent, and it was too soon for her husband and children to be back. Could it be one of the dogs? No—her husband had taken them with him. Just then, the door-flap was pushed aside, and Alet looked up from her sewing to see a strange woman she had never seen before stepping into the tent. She did not sit down—but just stood near the door, where the light was weakest. Alet could scarcely see her face, partly because it was in the shadows, and partly because the woman held a scarf over most of her face, as though to keep out the cold.

'You are surprised at my visit,' the woman said quickly, before Alet could speak. 'I have come to—help you. I know that for weeks now you have been sewing many new coats

for your family. And today you have been here alone—
sewing, sewing all day. Now you are tired. But still you
have not finished your own winter coat. And the sky is
heavy with more snow. *I* will sew for you. You can sleep,
and meanwhile I will sit up all night and sew. In the morning
you will see that—everything is finished.'

There was no harm in the *words*—but Alet did not like her
strange visitor's *voice*, which sounded to her both hard and
somehow menacing. She decided to pretend to do as the
woman said—but only pretend.

'I will be glad if you will sew for me,' she said. 'It is true
that I am tired. I will put the night-tent in position, and
sleep.'

So saying, she stood up and pulled across the piece of
material which was strung on a string at the back of the
tent. This was pushed aside during the daytime, but at night
it hung down from the top of the tent to the floor. Behind
this night-tent, as it was called, the parents slept, while their
children slept in the other part of the big tent.

Alet lay down on her reindeer-skin and kept very still.
But, through a little hole in the material, she could see her
strange visitor. After a while, the woman sat down near the
light, and took up Alet's coat. She took off her scarf—and
started to sew. But, it was not her *hand* she moved up and
down with each stitch that she took, it was her *head*! Alet
saw how her head bobbed up and down, surprisingly
quickly—and she saw *why*! The woman was sewing with
her NOSE! And her nose *shone* in the light. It was made of
metal! *Then* Alet knew whom her visitor was—Iron-Nose!

She had heard horrible tales about Iron-Nose from Lapp
woman who came from other parts of Lappland. How she
only appeared to women who were all alone, offered to

sew for them, then attacked them in the morning with her sharp iron-nose which had given her her name. How she bent over them when they were asleep, and struck them over and over gain in the chest and heart with her iron-nose!

Alet trembled as she realised how very dangerous her visitor was. Whatever was she to do? She moved slightly, as she lay there behind the night-tent, and as she moved her hand touched something very hard. She looked down to see what it was and found that it was a big piece of thick tin, which she had not yet melted to make thread for her embroidery. This gave her an idea.

Very, very quietly, she managed to pick up the thick piece of metal and then slowly, very slowly, placed it carefully over her chest. It was well hidden by her dress and, although she could not tie it on, Alet knew that it would not slip as long as she stayed still. She did not dare fall asleep, but kept a close watch on Iron-Nose, who went on sewing all night, for hours and hours, looking up every now and then, through the smoke-hole at the top of the tent, to see if it was still night. It began to get light—and lighter!

Suddenly, Iron-Nose threw down the reindeer-skin coat she had been sewing, and shouted, 'Now, *now* it is no longer night, NOW I can attack you and take your embroidered belts and collars I have heard so much about!'

She rushed full-speed at Alet, and struck hard at her chest with her iron-nose. But it was not Alet who was hurt, it was herself! Her iron-nose was *knocked off* by the piece of metal and it fell to the floor of the tent! Alet saw it knocked off. Then she saw Iron-Nose disappear into thin air before her very eyes. So quickly did it happen that Alet only just heard her mutter, 'My nose, my iron-nose! This Alet Sirma has finished me—for ever!'

Alet got up and looked at the coat which her unwelcome visitor had sewn all night. All the seams which Iron-Nose had sewn had come undone, her stitches had all come loose.

When her husband and children came back a few days later, she had finished her winter coat, and she knew that *her* stitches would last as long as the coat did. Her family listened in amazement as she told them of the strange visitor she had had in their absence, and she showed them the iron-nose to prove it. And, many times after that, Alet Sirma had to retell the story of how the tin she used for her embroidery saved her from Lappland's dreaded Iron-Nose, who was never seen again after that day.

Shaman Andreas aimed his arrow carefully at Stallo

26

Shaman against Stallo

AMONGST the earliest tales which are told of Lappland, there are many about Lapp sorcerers or shaman, and many others about Stallo, who could also work a wicked kind of sorcery of his own. Not only were there different kinds of shaman, depending on how many different kinds of sorcery he could work, but there were also various kinds of Stallo. These differed from each other very greatly in the manner in which they came into being in the first place. The main difference, of course, was that one kind of Stallo was made out of peat-turf by a Lapp who wanted a Stallo of his own, aided by a shaman who called it into life, whereas another kind of Stallo was made out of the Lapp himself, by himself, by varying means in different parts of Lappland. But, whatever kind of Stallo, and whatever kind of shaman, they could *all* work Lapp sorcery, of different kinds. Very seldom, however, did they try to work it on each other, for they were usually too busy working sorcery on other people.

But there is *one* story of a Stallo who tried to work his sorcery on a shaman. He probably thought that he was sure to win, because that particular shaman was not a shaman *all the time*; he only worked magic very occasionally, when he absolutely needed to for an important reason.

Because of this, not everyone knew that he *was* a shaman. But he managed to outwit the Stallo, as we shall see.

Now the shaman's name was Andreas Baiva, and he came from a very famous Lapp family indeed. Their name, 'Baiva', meant 'Sun', and the strength of the sun seemed to have been given to the men of the Baiva family, who had become famous all over Lappland for their ability to lift heavy objects higher, or push them farther, than other Lapps could.

Shaman Andreas was a nomadic Lapp with a fine herd of reindeer, which he kept in the mountains above Vadsø. One day, he decided that it was time to take some of his reindeer-skins into Vadsø and sell them, or rather exchange them, for various items of food which his family needed. This he could do with a fixed-dwelling Lapp, whose family had had to give up their nomadic life in the mountains because their reindeer herd did not prosper, but just became fewer and fewer.

They had moved to Vadsø and become sea-Lapps, fishing from small boats, both for their own needs and for sale. In time they had begun to buy reindeer-skins from the other Lapps who came down to Vadsø, and then sell them to other people, both fixed-dwelling Lapps like themselves, and others, non-Lapps. Later still they had begun to buy foods of various kinds, and re-sell them, mostly to mountain Lapps. It was very useful for these mountain Lapps to be more or less certain of being able to find a buyer for the reindeer-skins they took into Vadsø, and also to obtain the food and other supplies they needed at the same place.

Shaman Andreas Baiva was amongst the mountain Lapps who dealt with them, although he did not really like the Siggo family, especially Uldarak Siggo, who was now the head of the family, and the person to talk to if one wanted to buy or sell anything. He did not know *why* he disliked Uldarak, but somehow he had always done so and the feeling grew each time they met. Now, this particular time, he took his reindeer-skins down to Vadsø as usual. Uldarak Siggo looked at them all closely, to see if they were in good condition, and then agreed to take them all, as usual too. And Shaman Andreas chose the various items of food which he needed—all just as usual. But this time, when they had concluded their business, and Shaman Andreas was about to leave, Uldarak Siggo did not just say goodbye and wish him a safe journey back to his family, as he usually did.

Instead of doing this, he suddenly turned to Shaman Andreas and said, 'The menfolk of your family are all supposed to be much stronger than us other Lapps, but I wonder how high they can jump? I will bet you that I, Uldarak Siggo, can jump higher than you, Andreas Baiva!'

Shaman Andreas was surprised, both at the words and at the sneering tone in Uldarak's voice.

'I will accept your bet,' he said quietly. 'But how shall we prove it? And when?'

Uldarak led the way to where his boat lay, upturned, near the water.

'This boat has been newly painted with tar,' he said. 'That is why it is upside down. It is not yet dry. As you can see, it is a big boat. Now I will bet you that *you* cannot jump over it without getting tar on your clothes, but that *I* can! And, when I win the bet, I shall also win back all the things you have just bought from me. If you should win, you will also win back your reindeer-skins. But you will *not* win, you will see!'

Shaman Andreas readily agreed to jump over the boat, and he had to agree to the rest of the bet too, even though he thought it need not have been added. Uldarak told him to jump first. So Shaman Andreas walked back a distance from the boat, turned, ran fast towards it, and jumped. When he came down on the other side, he looked at his clothes to see if there was any tar on them, but there was none.

Then it was Uldarak's turn. He jumped very well, but not quite well enough. For, when he looked at his clothes afterwards, there was tar on the lower edge of the material. Uldarak was speechless with rage! Then he began to search and research Shaman Andreas' clothes, to see if he could not find a tiny trace of tar somewhere. But there was really none.

His rage increased when he had to give back to Shaman Andreas all the reindeer-skins. But that was his own fault; he should not have added that extra condition to the bet. And already he began to plot revenge! As Shaman Andreas left, Uldarak Siggo called after him, 'Your legs have won *this* bet for you, but wait until next year! I promise you that next year you will have more need of your legs than ever before!'

Shaman Andreas went back to his family in the mountains, and told them what had happened to him in Vadsø. And he remembered Uldarak's parting words, although he did not know what they might come to mean.

Several months went by and nothing happened. Then the spring came, and Shaman Andreas moved with his wife and two daughters on the Great Trek with their reindeer down to a place on the coast, just west of Vadsø, where they went every year at the same time. And Uldarak Siggo, in Vadsø, heard that they had arrived. It was what he had been waiting for.

He needed a Stallo to defeat Shaman Andreas, and revenge the bet of the year before. But *he* wanted to be the one who took this revenge. So there was only one possible thing to do. He had to make a Stallo *out of himself*.

To do this, Uldarak walked backwards around the church in Vadsø, from one hour before midnight until one hour after midnight. This he did again the next night, but in the opposite direction. On the third night he repeated it, but this time, in addition to walking backwards, he continually muttered, 'Take away the name I was given. I will no longer be Uldarak Siggo. I will be Stallo! Take away the name that is written in the church register, my name shall be Stallo!'

And, exactly one hour after midnight on the third night, he *did* become Stallo, with all Stallo's ways and special sorcery.

The very next day, he went to the place where Shaman Andreas had his reindeer. He found him busy amongst the herd. The first thing Stallo did was to make himself invisible, and the second thing was to w–h–i–s–t–l–e ... Now, the sound of a Stallo w–h–i–s–t–l–e was very different from the sound when an ordinary Lapp whistled, and everyone knew this. So, when Shaman Andreas, busy with his reindeer, suddenly heard a long-drawn-out w–h–i–s–t–l–e, he knew at once it was STALLO. And he also knew that the only person who could hear a Stallo w–h–i–s–t–l–e was the one whom that Stallo was out to destroy. Since *he* had heard it, it must be *him* the Stallo was after. But where was Stallo?

Shaman Andreas moved out from amongst the reindeer, and looked around him in every direction. But he could see nothing. Then it came again, that long, peculiarly menacing w–h–i–s–t–l–e, but this time it was nearer, and much louder.

M

163

And frightening, very frightening! Shaman Andreas began to move away from the place the sound had come from. He moved faster and faster, and soon began to run as fast as his legs would carry him. Then, suddenly, he remembered what Uldarak Siggo had said to him the year before, '—I promise you that, next year, you will have more need of your legs than ever before!' So the Stallo was Uldarak, and he had made his threat come true.

Well, there was one thing that Stallo did not know, and that was that the nomadic Andreas Baiva was also a shaman, and could work Lapp sorcery of his own. Shaman Andreas began to lose his fear of Stallo and to think what he could do to outwit and defeat him.

'First, I will show him that my legs can give me all the help I need *and* make him use his own! And then I will find a way to put an end to him.'

With that, Shaman Andreas wished that his legs should be given the same speed as those of a fully-grown wild reindeer in full flight. At once they were, and Shaman Andreas ran—ran—ran—until he had gone a very long way. Then he stopped, to find out whether he could hear Stallo. For quite a while there was no sound. Then all at once he heard Stallo's special w-h-i-s-t-l-e again, from not so far behind him.

Hastily, Shaman Andreas wished that his legs should now be given the same speed as those of a young wild reindeer calf, because when such a calf is at the age that its fur begins to moult and change to a thick winter coat, then it is so swift that nothing without wings can catch it. And at once, with the swiftness of a young wild reindeer calf, Shaman Andreas *ran—ran—ran—* until he was sure that he had at last left Stallo far behind.

By now he was quite near the place where he had his tent in winter, and he knew the territory well, every mountain, lake, and stone for miles around. Nearby, there were two lakes, and between them was a narrow strip of water, connecting them to each other. In the middle of this strip of water, just below the surface, there was a large stone which could not be seen, because the water was so calm and always covered it. But Shaman Andreas knew it was there. He had often jumped over from one side to the other by first stepping on the stone.

Now he ran quickly to the place, jumped on the stone, and over onto the other side. Then he ran to one of the lakes and around the edge of it, until he came to the middle, which was wide across. There he waited. Some considerable time afterwards, he saw Stallo appear on the opposite bank of the lake.

'So there you are at last!' he called out. 'I have been waiting for you. Your legs are not as good as mine, but at least you are visible now. It seems that you cannot *jump as high*, nor *run as fast* as I can. Let me see if you can at least jump *as far* as I have.'

When he heard this, Stallo became so angry that he did not stop to think what he was doing. In a blind fury, he took a running jump from his side of the lake, but even with the help of some Stallo sorcery, he didn't get any farther than the middle. As he went feet first into the water, Shaman Andreas watched him from the other side, then took his bow, which he used for hunting, and always carried with him. He spanned an arrow across it, and aimed it at Stallo. But Stallo jumped up so high in the water that the arrow just went between his feet. Shaman Andreas spanned another arrow, and aimed again. Again Stallo jumped up in the water, and this time the arrow went between his knees. But now Shaman Andreas knew what to expect.

Slowly, he took a third arrow. Carefully, he spanned it, and aimed it, not where Stallo was, but where he expected him to jump to. Stallo did jump, and this time the arrow got him! He sank to the bottom of the lake, and so saved Shaman Andreas the trouble of burying him, which he would have had to do otherwise.

As he made his way back to his reindeer, Shaman Andreas remembered how his father had insisted on teaching him the special shaman Lapp sorcery. He had taught him in secret, and Andreas had very seldom had need of the help of sorcery before. That was why no one knew that he was a shaman—not even his own wife and daughters. If Uldarak Siggo had known, he would probably have been more careful. But it is because he did *not* know that the Lapps have any story to tell of a clash between a Stallo and a Shaman, with their different kinds of Lapp sorcery. And even this one story was not told until Andreas Baiva was an old man. He told it to his only grandson, on the day he started to teach him the secrets of the age-old shaman sorcery. And, through his grandson's descendants, the story has been handed down to us.

27

Family feud in Kvikkjokk

In the Lapp village of Kvikkjokk, in Swedish Lappland, there once lived two families who had disliked each other for several generations. No one could remember exactly how the feud between the Pirak family and the Spik family had started. But one thing was certain. Ever since a number of Lapps built themselves fixed-dwellings by the Kvikkjokk river, and settled down there, these two families had been hard against each other. Both families were semi-nomadic; that is, they lived in Kvikkjokk during the whole winter, but moved with their reindeer on the big spring migration, and again on the autumn migration.

Now, no matter how many reindeer a Lapp has, he remembers every one of them if he has branded them himself with his own mark. To other people, all reindeer look very much alike. But not to a Lapp. The nomadic owner of a reindeer herd has a truly phenomenal memory as regards his animals. He remembers how many males and females, how many one-year-olds, two-year-olds, three-year-olds, etc., how many light-coloured or dark-coloured (all the way from the pure white ones to the black ones, both of these latter very rare), how many have been specially trained to pull sledges, as well as a lot of other things such as the shape of the various reindeers' horns, etc.

The end of the spring migration marks the beginning of the time when the little calves are born. The Lapp who owns the mother-reindeer brands the new calf as soon as possible, but at the end of the migration the reindeer all wander freely over quite a large area, and if the calf is born during this time, it may be the end of summer before the Lapp owner finds it. But he knows *how many* calves still have to be branded, and at the time of the round-up of all the herds, in autumn, each owner looks until he finds that many calves. They are still small enough to stay close to their mothers, so it is not difficult.

So, every autumn, the Pirak family would count their new calves. And every autumn, there were *too few* of them. Then they knew that, once again, members of the Spik family must have looked for the calves during the summer and put *their* brandmark on them, thus stealing them for their own herd.

Or, when the time came around for the Spik family to slaughter some reindeer to provide meat for themselves and to have some to sell to others, as well as to give them fur for clothing, every year they found that some of the best animals which they had intended for this purpose were just simply missing. Not to be found anywhere amongst the herd. Then they knew that the Pirak family must have found them, and slaughtered them 'by mistake'.

(Of course, no real mistake was possible, because of the brandmark on each animal's ear. And if any reindeer was ever slaughtered 'by mistake', the first part of it which disappeared was the ear, with its tale-telling mark.)

Sometimes, things happened the other way round. It was the Spik family who could not find enough calves, and the Pirak family whose best, grown reindeer were missing.

There were all kinds of other incidents too: sledges which broke down suddenly and unexpectedly, dogs which were sent to bark at a herd of reindeer and send the animals running wildly in the wrong direction, etc. So every year the bad feeling between the two families got stronger and stronger. It had reached bitter and outright enmity by the time Lanni Pirak and Kuono Spik were each the head of their respective families.

Lanni had a large family to be the head of, for he and his wife had no less than seven children: four boys and three girls. This meant that there were always enough people to hold watch over the reindeer *and* to help with the work at home, cooking, making clothes, curing reindeer skins, etc.

But Kuono had only one child, a daughter. So this meant that he had to hire other people as herdsmen to watch his reindeer. This was expensive, of course, but it was quite unfair that he should blame Lanni Spik for the whole matter. But blame him Kouno did.

To him, anything at all that went wrong with the Spik family's affairs must be because of interference by the Pirak family. Missing reindeer, lack of children—Kuono blamed Lanni for everything. And he began to threaten Lanni about his children.

'Seven of them you have,' he sneered, 'seven different accidents can happen to them. Many things are possible—things that cannot be explained! Just seven accidents, in the dark forests, on the deep lakes, or up in the high mountains, and you would have none left. None—none!'

Lanni knew that these were not empty words. In the wide, endless spaces of Lappland, where there might be no other living being for hundreds of miles, all kinds of accidents were indeed possible. A number of Lapps had just simply disappeared whilst journeying from one place to another; their families had never seen nor heard of them again. Had an avalanche of stones rolled down on them? Had they been attacked by bears or wolves? Had they frozen to death in a sudden, violent snowstorm? No one knew.

So Lanni began to be terribly afraid of what Kuono might cause to happen to one of *his* children—or indeed *all* of them, if he carried out his threat in full. But what could he do to stop him? For a long time he could think of no way at all to make sure Kuono did not harm his children. And with each day his anxiety increased. But at last something happened which gave him a chance to prevent Kuono from ever turning his threats into action.

Not far from the village of Kvikkjokk was a place where many beavers lived by the river. There were so many of them that they had become almost a pest, so every year the Lapps from Kvikkjokk tried to catch some of them, to keep their numbers down. Beaver fur was also a welcome addition to help keep them warm in the bitterly cold Lappland winters.

One day, Lanni decided that the time had again come around for him to begin beaver hunting. He gathered together the things that he would need, and set off along the banks of the river until he came to the right place. But, when he got there, he saw that someone else had had the same idea, for one of the nets was already in position. No matter, he would go a little farther along the river, for there were beavers in several different places along this particular stretch of water.

Still, he couldn't help wondering who the other Lapp hunter was. Perhaps it was one of his friends. If so, they could share a fire and a hot drink, as well as having someone to talk to while they were waiting to see whether any beavers went into their nets.

He could see the smoke from a fire as it curled up into the air, so he began to walk in that direction. And as he walked, he noticed a piece of rope which lay on the ground, leading from the net which he had seen in the water up towards the place where he could see the fire. This was curious. He had not gone very far, when he suddenly saw clearly the person to whom the net and the rope belonged. It was Kuono Spik!

Lanni stopped immediately, and was glad that a boulder hid him from Kuono's view. He saw Kuono put some more wood on the fire, remove most of his outer clothing, and lie down, right beside the fire, to sleep, placing the clothing over him. And he saw too what Kuono did before he slept. He took the other end of the rope, and attached it to a thick stick near him. Then he pulled it slightly, and Lanni heard a bell ringing. Then he understood what that rope was for.

If a beaver got caught in the net whilst Kuono was asleep, this would tug the rope which was attached to it, and that would make the bell ring and wake Kuono in time to hurry down before the beaver got out of the net. The Lapp hunters always had to hurry, because beavers had been known to bite their way through nets, with their exceptionally sharp teeth. And suddenly Lanni realised that he had here an opportunity to outwit his enemy and safeguard his children.

He waited until Kuono was asleep. Then he tugged hard on the rope. The bell rang. Kuono awoke with a start, stood up quickly, and hurried down to the water. Just as quickly, Lanni hurried up to the place where Kuono had slept, threw all his outer clothes on the fire, and hurried back to hide.

Kuono found, of course, nothing in the net, and he thought the beaver must have found some way of escaping. When he went back to his fire and saw that all his clothes were burning on it, he thought that he must have stood up in such a hurry, when he heard the bell ring, that he had carelessly caused his clothing to land on the nearby fire. He was very annoyed with himself, but he decided to go on with his beaver hunting anyway, so as to have something to show for his trouble. So he threw some more wood on the fire, and went back to sleep.

Lanni waited patiently until he was sure that Kuono really was very sound asleep. Then he again tugged on the rope. Again the bell rang. Kuono awoke, stood up quickly, and ran down to his net. Lanni raced up hill again, and this time he put out Kuono's fire. Then he again hid himself.

Kuono was very puzzled when he again found nothing in the net, and then, when he went back uphill and found that his fire had gone out, he became angry. For he suddenly realised that all these events had not happened on their own.

'Lanni Pirak!' he called out into the night, 'If it is *you* who have done all this, you will be sorry! For I will see that you too have an accident! Not just your seven children —but *you too*! I will finish the whole Pirak family!

It was a cold night, but as Kuono called out his threats to Lanni, the moon suddenly came out, bright and clear.

'The moon! The moon! Now you will see! Now you will see!' Kuono began to gabble. 'The moon will warm me —aha! I don't need the fire that you put out; the moon will give me all the warmth I need.'

Lanni listened in amazement as Kuono began to talk

directly to the moon. 'Moon, moon! keep me warm, keep me warm! So I may live to cause seven accidents to seven Pirak children—and an eighth to their father, aha! Moon, warm me, and help me finish off the whole Pirak family.'

But, of course, the moon gives *no* warmth, only light. So Kuono Spik froze from the cold, still uttering threats against Lanni Pirak and his family. The long feud between the two families had reached its climax.

Afterwards, the Piraks and the Spiks left each other alone. They even went out of their way to avoid each other. Descendants of the two families still live in Kvikkjokk. But nowadays the story of the long feud between them is just part of Kvikkjokk village history.

The magic drum, covered in weird signs and symbols

28

Shaman Slabrek and his magic drum

IN ancient times, no nomadic Lapp would start on any undertaking of importance before first trying to find out what its outcome might be. For example, if someone planned to go fishing in a distant lake, it was important to find out whether the lake was full of fish or not, and whether he was likely to be successful at catching many of them. Or, if a group of Lapps were planning a bearhunt, it was important to find the right day to start out; starting on a wrong day could mean very bad luck indeed—perhaps even somebody getting mauled by the bear. But *how* could they find this out? No *ordinary* Lapp could do it on his own. A *special* Lapp was needed, a Lapp sorcerer, a shaman. So every group of Lapps had at least one shaman who had learnt the age-old Lapp sorcery.

A Lapp village often had several shaman, for every family in it had many problems, large and small, which had to be decided upon before anything definite could be done about them. And every shaman had his magic drum, which gave him the answer, in its own way, to any question he asked it.

Now, in the village of Jukkasjervi, in Swedish Lappland, there once lived a shaman who was renowned far and wide for his gift of foretelling events and predicting what would happen to people. He was known as Shaman Slabrek, and he was such a powerful sorcerer that people were very much afraid of him, and were always careful not to make him angry.

One day, a nomadic Lapp named Bedir Allas, who was planning a journey with the whole of his family, sent for Shaman Slabrek to find out which would be the best day to start. For, if they chanced to leave on a wrong day— or even at the wrong time on the right day—there was no telling the number of misadventures which might befall them on the way. Shaman Slabrek came to the tent where the Allas family lived and brought his magic drum with him. Bedir Allas was dressed in his best clothes, and so was his wife, and their children, as befitted the occasion. Shaman Slabred was dressed in the same way—for each shaman wore the same kind of clothing as other Lapps; it was his ability to work various kinds of powerful sorcery and to use the magic drum that made him different from them.

'What is it that you wish to know?' asked Shaman Slabrek, when the Allas family had welcomed him into their tent.

'We must go on a journey to visit my cousin and his family in Parkajoki,' replied Bedir Allas, 'so we want to know *which* day to leave and at *what time* of day.'

Shaman Slabrek took out his magic drum, and everyone looked at it with a mixture of fascination and dread, as well they might, for it was an instrument of infinite mystery and power. They saw the tightly-stretched top of the magic drum, and could not take their eyes away from it. Made of taut reindeer-skin, it was covered in weird signs, figures and symbols, which only a shaman could interpret. The wooden sides were decorated in a strange pattern, too, and hung with fox-bones, bear-claws, and wolf-teeth.

Abruptly, Shaman Slabrek fell to his left knee, placed the magic drum on his right knee, and took a hammer, made of reindeer-horn, in his right hand. Bedir Allas made a sign, and everyone fell to their knees too. They could not stand if a shaman was kneeling. But, even as they knelt, they kept their eyes riveted on the mysterious symbols on the magic drum.

Shaman Slabrek put a small brass ring on the top of the drum, in the middle. (Everyone knew that brass, the same colour as the sun, was a sacred metal.) Then he hit the top of the drum, with the hammer. The brass ring jumped. Shaman Slabrek hit the drum again—and again—and again. Each time the ring jumped slightly and moved from the sign it had been placed upon in the middle, to one of the others, first in one direction, then another. At last it came to rest upon one particular symbol, and would not move away from it, even though Shaman Slabrek hit the drum several times. He stopped, and looked at Bedir Allas.

'Your journey must not begin until the eighth day from today,' he said. 'The drum has indicated dangers for every day until then. I have not asked the drum what these dangers are, for it is not necessary. There are many possibilities. It is spring, and the ice might crack just as you were crossing over a lake, for instance. It is enough that you know you should not begin your journey until the eighth day from now.'

'Yes, that is enough,' agreed Bedir Allas. 'But, would you now ask the drum *what time of day* we must start?'

Shaman Slabrek replaced the brass ring on the top of the drum, in the middle, and hit it hard several times. This time the ring jumped straight to one certain symbol, and remained there, no matter how often the hammer hit the top.

'You must leave at sunrise,' said Shaman Slabrek to Bedir Allas, 'exactly at sunrise on the eighth day.'

Bedir Allas nodded. 'There is one more thing troubling me,' he said. 'We cannot do the journey from Jukkasjervi to Parkajoki in one day, even if we start at sunrise. It will take us several days, and in between we shall need to stop, eat, and sleep. So we shall need to know, each evening, just *when* we should stop or whether it would be better, for some reason, not to stop at all, but to continue travelling through the night, and rest the next morning. Only a shaman can tell us what we need to know. Then, too my cousin lives some distance outside of Parkajoki, and I would have to send quite a long way for a shaman when we start to plan our journey back to Jukkasjervi at the end of our visit to my cousin. So I would ask you if it is possible for you to come with us. Only then would I feel certain that our journeys will be successful, and without danger.'

Shaman Slabrek again consulted his drum, and when the brass ring landed on one of the signs and definitely stayed there, he said, 'It *is* possible. I will come with you.'

Bedir Allas was very relieved to hear this news, and re- solved to pay Shaman Slabrek well for the advice he had already given, and that which he would give during the coming journey and the return. The rest of his family were both relieved and appalled, for the thought of having a powerful shaman constantly with them for such a long time was as frightening in some ways as it was reassuring in others. There was no need for Bedir Allas to tell his children that they would have to be on their best behaviour and not offend Shaman Slabrek in *any* way; they already realised this, without being told.

Exactly at sunrise on the morning of the eighth day, they

set off, each one with a reindeer and sledge of his own, but all joined together in single-file. In the front sledge, with the lead-reindeer, sat Bedir Allas, and in the next sledge came Shaman Slabrek with his magic drum. They travelled all day across wide expanses of white snow and over many frozen lakes. And in the evening Shaman Slabrek consulted his drum, and found the right time for them to stop. Next morning they continued their journey all day and all through the following night, for the magic drum had indicated that it would be unlucky for them to stop until morning. After several days, they reached Parkajoki and then the place beyond it where Bedir's cousin lived.

His name was Nalta Orpus, and although he was very glad to see Bedir and his family, whose visit, of course, he had not been expecting, nevertheless there was something worrying him very much, and this threatened to dim the pleasure of the visit for everyone. The trouble was that Nalta's wife, Sarat Orpus, was ill, and had been for some time. And no one had been able to find out what was the matter with her.

'I shall have to send for a shaman,' Nalta told Bedir. 'Perhaps a magic drum could tell us why she is ill.'

'But we have Shaman Slabrek with us,' explained Bedir. '*He* will be able to tell you today, what to do for Sarat.'

Nalta was very glad to hear this, and when the matter had been explained to Shaman Slabrek, he immediately took out his magic drum. Everybody went into the tent where the sick Sarat lay on a pile of reindeer-skins, and Nalta told her that a shaman from Jukkasjervi was going to ask his magic drum what was the matter with her. Sarat watched silently as Shaman Slabrek knelt on his left knee, the magic drum on his right knee, and the hammer in his right hand. The top of the drum, with its weird symbols and figures, was very close to her face, and this unexpected nearness frightened her into expectant silence.

Shaman Slabrek hit the top of the drum with his hammer several times in rapid succession. The brass ring began to jump—jump—jump—but not very far. It stayed close to the place in the middle where it had been put. Shaman Slabrek stopped and looked at Nalta.

'The signs are good,' he said, 'so your wife will live. She will not die from this sickness, whatever it is. Now, I will try to find out what is the matter with her. But that is much more difficult, and may take a long time.'

Sarat watched anxiously as the brass ring again began jumping each time Shaman Slabrek hit the drum with the hammer. But this time it behaved very strangely: jumping wildly about all over the top, touching many of the magic symbols, but not coming to rest on any of them. Several times Shamen Slabrek stopped completely, replaced the brass ring in the middle, and started again with a new, silent question to the drum. Everyone in the tent was absolutely silent too, not daring to make the slightest sound, as they watched the brass ring jumping and jumping amongst the symbols, refusing to stop on any of them. *Whatever could this mean?*

At last, Shaman Slabrek stopped and turned slowly to Nalta. 'Your wife must have some extraordinary sickness of which I do not know the name,' he said. 'I have asked the magic drum whether she has any of the many, many sicknesses whose name I know, and in each and every case, the answer has been *no*. And until I find out what is the matter with her, I cannot ask the drum what must be done to cure her.'

This was bad news, and no one knew what to say. Poor Sarat looked worse than ever.

Shaman Slabrek considered what to do next. At last a new idea occurred to him. He replaced the brass ring on top of the magic drum, and began to hit it with the hammer. The ring soon settled on one place, on one symbol—and would not move from it. Nalta watched closely. Whatever question Shaman Slabrek had just asked the magic drum, he had got a definite answer. Now the ring began to jump anew, as Shamen Slabrek replaced it once more and hit the drum hard, several times in quick repetition. After awhile, it landed on one of the figures, and stayed there.

'Aha, now I understand!' said Shaman Slabrek to Nalta. 'It is not a real illness at all that your wife is suffering from. You have an enemy, and this enemy has paid a shaman to send demons to plague your wife, and make her ill. *That* is what is the matter with her! But we cannot do anything to help her until we know *who* this enemy is.'

'An *enemy*!' exclaimed Nalta. 'Oh, I can tell you who that is, for there is only one possible person. It can only be a man named Vuolob Biti, who lives near here in Parkajoki.'

Shaman Slabrek turned back to his magic drum, and was soon able to tell Nalta, 'Yes, it *is* the man you think it must be, who has sent the demons.'

'Now that we know that, what must we do to cure Sarat?' asked Nalta anxiously.

Shaman Slabrek again consulted his magic drum in the same way as before—but, for a long time, it seemed reluctant to give an answer. Sarat and Nalta watched more and more worriedly as Shaman Slabrek hit the drum harder and *harder*—faster and *faster*. At long last he stopped.

'It is as I thought,' he said, 'there is only *one* thing you

can do. You must send *more powerful* demons to fight the
ones that your enemy has sent, and defeat them. Only a
very powerful shaman can do this. *I* can send these demons
for you—and then your wife will recover. But you must
tell me if this is what you wish.'

Nalta looked at Bedir, and Bedir said, 'You are *lucky* to
have here a shaman who is powerful enough to send demons
which will be strong enough to defeat the others, and cure
your wife.'

So Nalta hesitated no longer, but asked Shaman Slabrek to
do everything that was necessary to make his wife well again.

'This will take several days,' said Shaman Slabrek, 'but,
before we leave here on our return journey to Jukkasjervi,
your wife will be cured.'

Bedir and his family stayed with Nalta and Sarat for
nearly three weeks, and during the whole of the first week
poor Sarat almost seemed to be more ill than ever. She
tossed and turned, day and night—moaning and crying out
all the time. But at last, one day, this suddenly stopped
completely. Sarat lay still, and slept peacefully. The next
day she got up, and was as well and healthy as she had
ever been. And she stayed completely cured.

Nalta, of course, was very happy and thankful, and he
gladly paid Shaman Slabrek a handsome sum of money for
having used his powers of sorcery to consult the magic
drum, and then to send the demons away. Later, Shaman
Slabrek was able to tell Bedir which was the best day for
them to start on their return journey. There were no
mishaps on the way, and in a few days they were safely back
in Jukkasjervi.

They had been away for over a month, and many people
from the village were waiting to consult Shaman Slabrek.

One Lapp, whose reindeer had been doing badly lately, wanted the magic drum to indicate in which direction he should take his herd to be sure of finding a place where plenty of reindeer moss was growing. Another Lapp wanted the drum's help on the important matter of finding the right hiding-place for his money, a place so safe and secure that no other Lapp would come across it. Yet a third wanted the magic drum to help decide which of three Lapp girls would be the most suitable bride for his youngest son.

All over Lappland, as each season came and went, every shaman would be called upon to give advice on these and a hundred other questions. So, whether in Norwegian, Swedish, Finnish, or Russian Lappland, the busiest person in any Lapp tribe was almost certain to be its most renowned shaman, with his strange magic drum.

29

Why dogs are the Lapps' favourite animals

THERE are all kinds of animals and birds in Lappland. Most of them have been there as long as the Lapps themselves —some even longer. And around them have grown many different sayings and superstitions, some of which can still be heard today.

Take the raven, for example. This black bird has always had a strong, raucous voice, quite different from the sweet voices of other birds. The Lapps of long ago used to wonder what it was saying with its ugly, insistent tones. It seemed to make the most noise of all when it was having food, especially when eating frogs.

Now the Lapps disliked the slimy frogs very much, and they thought that frogmeat probably tasted very nasty, even to a raven. So they came to the conclusion that what the raven was saying must be this: 'Kra-a—kra-a—frogmeat is horrible—frogmeat is bitter—frogmeat is rancid! I'll never eat frogmeat again, I promise you.' But of course, the next time the raven was hungry, it *did* eat frogmeat again, just as before.

That is why, if someone has promised to do something, and they doubt that he will really do it, the Lapps say,

'First wait and see. It may well be only a raven-promise he has given.'

The cuckoo is another bird which has a most distinctive voice. But it is a pleasant one, even if unusual, and it heralds the coming of pleasant warm weather—not spring, as elsewhere, but early summer in Lappland, where the seasons are later. Although the Lapps have always been glad to hear the cuckoo, they used to believe that it was unlucky to hear one before they had eaten in the morning— and very, very unlucky indeed if a cuckoo should chance to alight on their own tent, and call out his cuckoo sound from there, just as they were getting up. This was only the case, however, for the *very first time* they heard the cuckoo, each year. After that, it did not matter how or when they heard it.

So each year, when the time came around again when they knew they could expect to hear the first cuckoo, every Lapp—man, woman, and child—was careful to put a piece of bread beneath his or her head when they went to sleep. Immediately they woke up in the morning, they would take this bread and eat it—even before they got up. After that it was not unlucky to hear the cuckoo, for they had already eaten something!

Dogs have always been favoured animals to the Lapps, and there is a reason for this. Long, long ago, when the Lapps were first trying to catch the thousands of reindeer which roamed freely in the mountains and forests of Lappland, they soon realised that they would need some kind of help. The reindeer were nervous and swift in flight, and it was impossible to round them up in sufficient numbers to start a separate herd for each Lapp. Yet it had to be done, for the Lapps needed reindeer-skins for clothing to keep them warm during the bitter winters, and meat to feed them; not to mention milk and cheese, all of which reindeer could provide them with.

But the help the Lapps needed was not so easy to get. There were no other human beings there but themselves, at that time. So, in desperation, they decided to ask some of the other Lappland animals to help them, and to reward them handsomely if they did so. The oldest and wisest Lapp amongst them was chosen to go to all the animals in turn, and see what they said. So off he set, and the first animal he encountered was a cow.

'Will you help us with our work in rounding-up the reindeer?' he asked.

The cow looked at him and answered, 'Moo! No, I won't! I have no time to help you, for I have not yet eaten enough to feel full.'

This answer made the old Lapp angry, and he thought to himself, 'The cow would have been well rewarded for its help, but now it shall be punished for thinking only of itself.'

So he said, 'You may keep on eating—but you will *never* feel full, from now on. Your jaws will always become tired from chewing—*chewing—c-h-e-w-i-n-g*, long before you are full. And it shall be the same for all those who come after you.'

That is why, even today, cows eat and eat continuously, only stopping to sleep, and as soon as they wake up again, they go straight back to eating.

The second animal that the old Lapp encountered was a hare, lying lazily on a sun-warmed stone.

'You who are so swift of foot, will *you* help us in our task of rounding-up the reindeer?' he asked.

The hare yawned. 'No, I can't help you. I'm thinking about building myself a home for the winter.'

This selfish answer made the old Lapp angry again, and he said, 'For the rest of your life, that's as far as you'll get—just *thinking* about getting a home for yourself! You will *never* get one built. Nor will any of those who come after you.'

That is why, even now, the hare sits miserably in the snow every winter, and says to itself, 'Oh, I should have built myself a home last summer, before the snow came back and covered everything. But *next* summer, *then* I'll build one—I will, I will!'

But, when the next summer does come, the hare just lies on a warm stone in the sun, as before, and thinks, 'Oh well, I lived through *last* winter, and *next* winter won't be any worse than that was!' So the hare never gets a home built.

The old Lapp kept walking along, and came to a river. At the edge of it was a fish, and when he saw it, the Lapp exclaimed, 'Oh, what a beautiful flounder!' He was going on to ask the flounder if it would give the help he was in need of but, even before he had time to get the question out, the fish had twisted its mouth sideways at him, and repeated after him, in a mocking voice, 'Oh—what a b-e-a-u-t-i-f-u-l f-l-o-u-n-d-e-r, he! he!'

No wonder the old Lapp got so angry at this that he said, 'You shall have a twisted mouth from now on—you, and all other fish that are like you!' That is why, still today, all flat fish have a mouth that is twisted sideways.

Again the old Lapp continued on his way, and the next animal he met was a bear.

'You who are the strongest and wisest animal in the

forests of Lappland, will you help us with the reindeer?'

'Oh, no, that I won't' answered the bear. 'I'm sleepy—so-o sleepy—and I'm just going to have a long sleep.'

'A long sleep indeed you shall have!' the old Lapp told him. 'Every winter from now on, you and all those who come after you will feel terribly tired, so tired that you will have to sleep through the entire winter. You'll get your long sleep—that I promise you!'

Which is why the bear still sleeps, or hibernates, all through the winter, and does not wake up until the spring.

At last the old Lapp met a dog.

'Will *you* help us with the reindeer?' he asked.

The dog looked up at the Lapp, gave a friendly bark, and then said, 'Yes, yes, I will help you!'

'Oh, thank you, thank you very much,' the old Lapp said gratefully. 'We will teach you to round-up the reindeer and bring them to us, and if you do it well, we promise to treat you well—you, and those who come after you. You shall be well fed, we will never mistreat you, and you shall be allowed to sleep in the warmth of the tent whenever the nights are cold.'

The dog agreed to this—and soon proved to be an excellent help to the Lapps.

That is why, even today, every nomadic reindeer owner has at least one dog of his own, sometimes more, each of which helps him with the difficult job of rounding-up his reindeer, which may have strayed miles away. And that is also why every Lapp dog is well treated and well fed, and allowed to sleep in the tent of the family it belongs to, instead of having to shiver out in the snow.

Backwards and forwards Sammul's sledge was pulled by a wolf!

30

'Backwards-and-forwards' Sammul

JUST outside the Lapp village of Arjeplog, in Swedish Lappland, there once lived a man who, when he spoke, talked in such a way that it was difficult to understand what he meant. He would stop in the middle of a sentence, change his mind about what he wanted to say, go back to the beginning again, speak so fast that the words tumbled out all jumbled up together, go back again to explain what he had just said, then suddenly forget what he had meant to continue with and stop altogether. His name was really Sammul Marak, but no one ever called him that. No, because of the strange way he talked, he was known as 'Backwards-and-Forwards' Sammul.

Children often made fun of him, and even grown-ups looked down on him, not only because of the strange way he spoke, but also because he had no reindeer of his own, and therefore had to hire himself out to other Lapps who had so many reindeer that they needed extra help in watching and herding them. People thought he was stupid— but he wasn't, he was just unlucky. Unlucky enough to be both very poor and to have a bad defect in his speech. Sometimes, whilst he was all alone, tending other people's reindeer, he would wonder whether anything might ever happen to change his luck for the better. And one day, something did!

It was late winter, and a lot of snow had fallen that year, which meant that the wolves could not find food, and would attack any stray reindeer they found. Every herd had to be watched all the time, to prevent any of the animals straying. 'Backwards-and-Forwards' Sammul was keeping watch over a small herd. He liked to be with the reindeer, because he didn't have to talk to them. Lightweight skis made it possible to move quickly, even in the deepest snow, and as he skied around the edge of the herd, two specially trained dogs helped him to turn back any stragglers.

At that time of year the daylight had returned to Lappland—and so had the sun. But at night it was still dark, unless the moon was out. 'Backwards-and-Forwards' Sammul was tired. He had been on watch for a long while and it was almost time for another herdsman to come and take his place and let him rest. His eyes too were tired, from straining for hours through the darkness to see the reindeer and follow where they went. That was why, when he saw something black moving around the edge of the herd, he at first thought it was one of the black dogs. Then he saw that the dogs were both only a few feet away from him, and *both* of them were standing absolutely still, necks craned forward, peering in the direction where he had seen the movement, fur bristling, and growling deep in their throats. If it was not one of the dogs, then there was only *one* other animal it could be—a wolf!

'Backwards-and-Forwards' Sammul began to ski towards the place where the wolf was, pushing himself along with the long stick he held in one hand, to increase his speed. Peering through the darkness, at first he could see only reindeer. They were all moving uneasily, running nervously first in one direction, then in another, sensing the nearness of their dreaded enemy, the wolf. Then he saw the beast: loping up and down, up and down, trying to separate one of the reindeer from the rest, the better to attack it.

At almost the same moment, the wolf saw him. It stopped moving, flattened itself to the ground, and watched him warily.

Now, 'Backwards-and-Forwards' Sammul was not a hunter. He was a herdsman—and this was the first wolf he had encountered. Of course he had a gun with him, and he knew how to use it. But it was too *dark* for him to be able to aim it properly. He stood there, the gun in his hand, not knowing quite what to do. He thought of trying to use his lasso, which he always had with him when on watch. But it was too dark for that too. The wolf seemed to sense his indecision. Instead of running off, it came nearer. Then nearer again, still keeping low to the ground.

And suddenly 'Backwards-and-Forwards' Sammul realised that the black beast of prey was getting into position to attack *him*! He did not have long to think how to defend himself, for the wolf, seeing that he kept so still, soon tensed itself and then sprang through the air, surprisingly high, straight towards him. 'Backwards-and-Forwards' Sammul did the only possible thing there was to do. He hit out hard at the wolf with the end of the gun which he was still holding. The blow caught it in mid-air, and when the wolf dropped at his feet, stunned but still alive, he realised that the hard gun must have struck it on the head and knocked it senseless.

Quickly, he took off his lasso, which hung around him in a coil over one shoulder and under the opposite arm. With it, he tied the wolf up, first fastening its jaws together so the beast would not be able to bite him—then its legs.

When it was thoroughly tied up, he wondered what to do with it next. Then he heard someone calling him, someone who was looking for him in the darkness. He knew that it must be the other herdsman whose turn it now was to watch over the herd.

For a moment he thought of telling him about the wolf. Then he thought better of it, for he knew that he would almost certainly get his words all mixed up again, and the other man would not understand what he meant. So, for the moment, he left the wolf where it was and hurried towards the approaching herdsman, whose name was Erke Labbas. Erke stopped to greet him briefly; then, after a few moments, began his watch over the reindeer, ski-ing around the herd. But the reindeer had by now moved away from the place where they had been before, and in the darkness Erke Labbas did not see the wolf, which was lying on the ground, tied up.

'Backwards-and-Forwards' Sammul was able to get back to the wolf, sling the beast over his shoulder, and start on his way back to Arjeplog, without Erke noticing anything at all. When he got home to his tent, he first tied the wolf to a tree, then refastened the ropes around it in such a way that its front legs were tied to its back ones. Its jaws he retied as before. So it could move around, but it could not bite nor run away.

After a good night's sleep, Sammul woke up, remembered about the wolf, and began to wonder what he was going to do with it. The most sensible thing, of course, would be to shoot it now that he could see to aim. He went out of the tent. The wolf did not seem as fierce as it had the night before. It was now really weak from hunger and just lay still, only moving its eyes to watch him.

On one of the branches of the tree to which the wolf was attached, there hung a reindeer harness, which 'Backwards-and-Forwards' Sammul had put there several days previously. It did not belong to him, because he had no reindeer of his own. But when he needed a reindeer and sledge to take him on a journey, which was not often, the Lapp whose herd he usually watched lent him one of his animals, with a sledge and harness. And he still had the harness from the last such occasion.

Suddenly, 'Backwards-and-Forwards' Sammul had a startling idea! 'I have no *reindeer* of my own, true enough,' he thought to himself, 'but I have a *wolf* of my own. *No one* else has that! I must not *shoot it. I must try to put a harness on it and train it to pull a sledge!*'

Pleased with his idea, he began to think out how to put it into action. First he went back inside the tent, got a good fire going, and cooked a meal of reindeer meat in rich reindeer broth. This meat was one of the few things that he usually had enough of, because the reindeer owners whose herds he watched often paid him with reindeer meat. When he had eaten, he took some of the bones, with bits of meat still clinging to them, and went outside with them. He threw them down in front of the wolf. The wolf cast itself at them. But because its jaws were tied, it could not seize them in its mouth.

'Backwards-and-Forwards' Sammul waited. When the wolf had exhausted itself, still without getting the meat, he went slowly towards it until he was close enough to loosen the rope around its jaws, without undoing it entirely. It almost seemed as though the wolf realised his intentions, for it made no move to pull away, nor to attack him. When he drew back again, it threw itself on the meatbones

o

and devoured them hungrily, crunching everything up in its strong teeth. When it had finished, the wolf turned round towards 'Backwards-and-Forwards' Sammul, who had stood near by, watching it. And for an instant, it looked straight at him. A strange look—part gratitude, part something else. And it made no protest when he took the harness and dropped it over its head, leaving it there for several minutes, nor when he again removed the harness, and retightened the rope around its jaws.

'Backwards-and-Forwards' Sammul was pleased and a little puzzled at the progress he had made in training the wolf. During the next three weeks, he repeated the same manoeuvre, whenever he was not away tending reindeer. He kept the wolf tied to the tree, but he fed it, and trained it to be used to the harness and to pull the sledge which he borrowed and attached to the harness. And all the time he talked to it, to get it used to his voice, and to obey easy commands. As he lived all by himself, some distance away from Arjeplog, he had no visitors. So he talked to no one, and no one knew anything about what he was doing.

Then there came a day when there was to be a wedding in the church at Arjeplog. It had been planned for some time, and 'Backwards-and-Forwards' Sammul, who was a distant relation of the bridegroom, was invited.

'You can borrow one of my reindeer,' said the Lapp whose herd he was watching at the time. 'The harness and sledge you have borrowed already.'

'Er—no, thank you,' said 'Backwards-and-Forwards' Sammul, politely. 'I have an animal of my own now to pull me.'

This was news to the herd owner, and he began to wonder whether his herdsman had stolen one of the animals from *his* herd. So he resolved to look at it closely when it got to the church. And he *did* look at it closely—but he was not the only one! Every Lapp in Arjeplog looked in amazement when 'Backwards-and-Forwards' Sammul swept up to the church in a sledge pulled by a *wolf*! He tied it up with all the other sledges—and he got more attention than the bride and groom! Everyone wanted to talk to him and ask him about the wolf, and in the general excitement and confusion it was some time before anyone realised that 'Backwards-and-Forwards' Sammul was *not* talking backwards-and-forwards any more, but just as clearly and understandably as other people. It was his fellow herdsman, Erke Labbas, who first noticed—and he was so startled that he almost started to talk backwards-and-forwards himself!

All this was so strange that people began to feel a new respect for the poor herdsman they had so often made fun of. There was no longer any reason to call him 'Backwards-and-Forwards' Sammul, so they started to use his real name, which was, of course, Sammul Marak. Sammul was delighted at the turn events had taken, but he was as puzzled as everyone else as to why he could now speak properly, instead of backwards-and-forwards as before.

It was not until the next day that he got an explanation. The wolf, that he had tied as usual to the tree when he returned to his tent after the wedding, was no longer there. In his place was a man, a Lapp whom Sammul had never seen before. He was wearing, not the costume of Arjeplog, but another costume from quite a different part of Lappland.

Seeing Sammul's uncomprehending expression, the

stranger said, 'Do not look for the wolf, Sammul Marak, for you will not find it. *I* was that wolf! For a shaman in my village turned me into a wolf, to revenge himself on my family. And I would have stayed a wolf for ever, if you had not saved me by giving me cooked meat. That was the *one* thing which could turn me back into a Lapp again. I could have changed myself back straight after the first meal you gave me, but I was so grateful to you, that I decided to wait and see whether I could help you better by staying a wolf for a while, first. When I realised what you were trying to do with the harness, I knew I was right.

'The night you first caught me, I heard Erke Labbas call you 'Backwards-and-Forwards' Sammul. But when you talked alone with me, you spoke as well as other people do. I thought that it might be because, for the first time in your life, you had something which no one else had. A wolf of your own!

'Now people will always be able to understand what you say, and will not make fun of you any more. And they will not look down on you any more, either, for I have so many reindeer in my herd that I am going to give you half of them, to start a herd of your own.'

Sammul grew more and more amazed with every word the stranger said. But he invited him inside his tent, to eat with him, and to tell him the whole story all over again. Later, the stranger left for his own part of Lappland.

But he was as good as his word—or even better. For when he sent Sammul the reindeer he had promised him— and there were many of them—he sent his sister along, too, to make sure that the animals got safely to the right person. His sister liked it in Arjeplog. And she liked Sammul Marak, too. So soon there was another wedding in the Arjeplog church.

From that time onwards, with a pretty wife and a fine reindeer herd of his own, Sammul was both lucky and well respected. He spoke slowly—but clearly. And no one ever again called him 'Backwards-and-Forwards' Sammul.

31

The bearhunt

THE first early snow had fallen and covered most of Lapp-land with a thin, light layer of white. There was not yet enough to ski on. But there *was* enough to see footprints in. One could tell where people, dogs, reindeer, had passed, from the traces they had left.

And in the region around Arvidsjaure, in Swedish Lappland, a Lapp named Apmut Tuolja was out, searching the white-covered earth with his sharp Lapp eyes, trained by years of experience. He was looking for one thing only—traces of BEAR. If he found any, this would be the start of a big bear-hunting ceremony and festival. For the bear was specially respected by the Lapps. Was it not the biggest, wisest, and strongest animal in Lappland? To hunt success-fully such a superior animal gave the hunter special prestige amongst his fellow Lapps.

Apmut Toulja had a great deal of prestige already, for he was one of the best bear hunters anywhere around Arvidsjaure. And early every winter, when the first snow fell, the old excitement of the bearhunt gripped Apmut anew. That was the time to look for traces, before the bears retired to their lairs to sleep all winter. Once they were asleep, they would make no traces which could help the hunters track them down. And *before* the first snow fell, their traces were not visible. So the hunters only had a short time for their search.

Of course, they did hunt bear in summer too, but this was so much more difficult that it only happened rarely.

Apmut walked and walked all day, over the terrain where he had found bears in the past. But it was not until the short hours of daylight were almost gone that he finally found what he was looking for. There at last were the unmistakable tracks of a huge bear! As quickly as possible, Apmut followed them. They led him first in one direction, then in another, sometimes even going round in a circle. But eventually the tracks came to an end. They just stopped suddenly, at a place where the snow on the ground stopped, in front of a cave in the rock. The tracks went up to the cave, but they did not come *out* of it again.

So Apmut knew that the huge bear was still inside the cave. And that it intended to make the cave its lair for the winter. Slowly he walked all around the outside of the cave, to 'ring the bear in', as this was called. Then he went away, back to Arvidsjaure.

He had done all he had set out to do that day: find the traces of a bear, track it to its lair, ring it in. Nothing more could be done for the moment. Nor indeed, during the whole of the coming winter. He would have to wait until the spring before the actual bearhunting could properly begin. For once in its lair, the bear would have settled into its winter hibernation, from which nothing could rouse it. The heavy winter snows would come, and then go again, before the bear awakened from its sleep.

'Let it stay in its lair,' Apmut thought to himself. 'It will not move away. I know where it is—and in the meantime, I can prepare for the hunt next spring.'

He would tell the other Lapps in Arvidsjaure about his bear, for he would need their help in catching it. Bear-hunting was a very big matter indeed, and no one man could manage it on his own. This bear was Apmut's, as he was the one who had found it, but the whole of the Arvidsjaure tribe would share in the bearhunting ceremony and festival.

'I will ask Birul to be the one to spear the bear,' decided Apmut. 'He did me the honour, last year, of making me the one to spear *his* bear.'

Birul Ruonga was Apmut's best friend, and always had been ever since they were both boys, learning about bearhunting from their fathers. And two years ago, Apmut's sister Kaja had married Birul, so now they were brothers-in-law.

It seemed a long time until spring. But at last, one day in April, it was decided that the right time had come for the bearhunt proper to begin. The most powerful shaman in Arvidsjaure had consulted his magic drum and declared that the signs were right for that particular day and that it would be a successful hunt. So the hunters set off for the lair.

At the head of them went Apmut, for it was his bear, and only he knew where the lair was. In his hand he carried a stick with a brass ring on it. Brass was a sacred metal to the Lapps, being the same colour as the sun, and was widely used in connection with the ceremonial hunting of the bear, to honour the powerful animal. After Apmut came the shaman, carrying his magic drum, for it might be necessary to consult both him and his drum during the hunt; so he had to be near to the two main hunters. Close after him came Birul Ruonga, to whom had been offered the honour of being the one to spear the bear. This was a job which needed considerable courage, and it was only offered to a man known to be both brave and bold. And, after these three main figures came the rest of the hunters, more or less in the order of their importance in the tribe.

No one spoke very much. There was, above all, ONE word which could *not* be uttered. This was the word 'BEAR'. The subject of all their thoughts should *never*, NEVER be called by his real name. To do so might be fatally unlucky. Instead, they referred to him, when at all, as 'Old Man Fur' or 'The Wintersleeper', and hoped fervently that if any bear chanced to overhear their conversation, it would not realise whom it was they were talking about. For, as a shaman had once said, 'These animals live in our land, so perhaps they understand our language!' So it was best to be careful, *very* careful, when talking about this wisest and most powerful beast.

When the hunters reached the lair that Apmut lead them to, they fixed two long poles across the narrow entrance to the cave, to make sure that the bear, once awakened, would not rush out at them full speed. This done, Birul took up position not too far away from the entrance, with his spear at the ready. Apmut stood a little further back and to one side, with his spear at the ready too, to be able to spring to his friend's help in case something went wrong. On the other side stood the shaman, with his magic drum.

At a sign from him, all the hunters began SHOUTING and YELLING at once, making as much noise as possible in order to wake the bear up from his long sleep (which by now, with the coming of spring, was much lighter than it had been during the dark winter months). For awhile nothing happened. Everyone *redoubled* his efforts, and Birul watched the cave entrance tensely and concentratedly. Surely that bear must soon come out to investigate what was causing such a noise?

Suddenly Birul saw two wicked-looking eyes, peering straight at him from a large head atop a huge body. How terribly *near* he was! And how deadly dangerous he looked! Birul's spear flew through the air, and the huge bear rolled over and lay still. All the hunters gathered round Birul to congratulate him on his aim. Then they dragged the bear out of the cave.

Even Apmut was surprised to see what a huge beast it was—quite the biggest he had ever seen, when it was stretched out full length. The shaman started to joik, which is the Lapp way of singing, and the song he sang was the Bearjoik—the song expressing gratitude to the dead bear for not having clawed anyone, nor damaged anyone's spear. All the hunters joined in this ceremonial Bearjoik. Then, in order to improve their luck on future bearhunts, they all shook their spears over the bear they had just defeated. When this was done, everyone helped to cover up the bear by piling spruce branches all over him.

His lair was not really very far from where they lived in Arvidsjaure, and they could have carried him home the same day. But everyone knew that this was never done. First there were a number of special ceremonies which had to be gone through at home with their families in Arvidsjaure. Only after this would it be safe and right to bring the bear down.

So they left the bear where it lay covered, and started off for home again. When they came almost to Arvidsjaure, near enough to be sure that the womenfolk would be able to hear them, Apmut and Birul led all the hunters in the joiking of another special Bearjoik, a song which told of their bearhunting feats, and their success. The womenfolk in the tents heard this special Bearjoik of victory and began in their turn to joik loudly too, a song to welcome back the bold, successful hunters. Perhaps the loudest joiker amongst the womenfolk was Kaja, for was she not the wife of one of the day's chief hunters, and sister to the other?

The Lapp women had not been idle whilst their men were away hunting. Now, after seeing to it that the hunters first had food, they decorated each man with their sacred metal, by putting small brass rings (which they had tied together on threads) around his neck, around one arm, and around one leg. All this was part of the bearhunting ceremony. The rest of that day, the hunters just rested.

It was not until the next day that they went back to get the bear. Some of them stayed behind in Arvidsjaure to prepare fuel for cooking the meat in huge cauldrons (all the actual cooking would be their job, too—not the womenfolk's), and to dig out a place where the bear's bones could later be ceremonially buried. Apmut took his best sledge to load the bear onto, and his strongest reindeer to pull it home. And he decorated both the sledge and the reindeer with brass rings. It took Apmut, Birul, and several others to load the huge, heavy bear onto the sledge, and then it took them most of the day to get the sledge back to Arvidsjaure.

Apmut walked ahead of his reindeer, leading it by the rein and helping it as much as he could, but it was spring, the snow was getting soft, and the heavily-laden sledge kept sinking down, slowing their progress. But they all knew that when they did get to Arvidsjaure there would be at least three days of feasting ahead of them, so they sang another joik as they made their way along. When they got back to their tents, the first thing they did was to skin the bear. The skin belonged entirely to Apmut, because he was the one who had originally found the traces of the bear, and tracked it to its lair.

But the meat belonged to everyone. And soon the big cauldrons were full of it. These should not be *too* full, however, for it was regarded as *very unlucky* if one of the cauldrons boiled over into the fire.

'I would rather have the danger of hunting the Winter-sleeper with my spear, than the responsibility of cooking his meat,' said Birul to Apmut.

Apmut agreed with his friend, for the cooking of the meat was no light and easy matter. Once the snow had been melted in the cauldron and the meat placed in with it, it would be unlucky to remove either, even if the cauldron threatened to boil over. And it would be just as unlucky to remove any wood from underneath the cauldron, to diminish the heat and stop it in that way from boiling over. No, bear meat was not as other meat. It had to be cooked in a special, ceremonial way. And in the process, *nothing*, once done, should be changed. No salt was put with it, although salt was always used with other meat, such as reindeer. And it should never be kept, or dried, as reindeer meat was, to use as a food reserve during the coming months. No, bear meat had to be all eaten up as soon as possible. So everyone in Arvidsjaure, man, woman and child, took part in each bear meat feast, no matter whose bear it was.

Apmut's bear was so huge that this particular feast went on for four days and nights, instead of the usual three. Everyone for miles around feasted on the plentiful meat.

At last there was nothing left but the bones. These everyone had been careful not to break, but to keep as intact as possible. The shaman put the bones in the hole which had been specially dug for them, and he placed each bone as nearly as possible next to the bones which had originally been together when the bear was alive. Then he covered the hole over again. All the hunters sang the last of the special Bearjoiks: the one thanking the bear for providing so much good food for them and their families.

Bearhunting was, of course, such a dangerous undertaking, that it was mostly the men's affair, from beginning to end. The womenfolk took only a small part in it. But now, after the days of feasting, there was one part of the bearhunting ceremony which belonged especially to them.

Apmut first took the skin of the bear, and attached it to a nearby tree. Then he called all the Lapp women, one at a time, out of the tents where they had stayed until that moment. Each woman had to tie something over her eyes first, so that she could not see anything. As each one came out of her tent, she was handed a stick from an alder tree and told to throw it in the direction where she thought the bearskin most probably was. None of the Lapp women could see anything, so alder sticks were soon flying through the air in all directions—most of them wide of the mark. Suddenly one stick landed right on the head of the bear!

Apmut looked to see who had thrown it and found that the one who was standing with her throwing arm still outstretched, her eyes still bound with a kerchief, was none other than his own sister, Kaja.

Now there was a special meaning to the throwing of the alder sticks. And as the shaman congratulated Kaja for the best throw, he also predicted that it would be *her* husband who found the first beartracks in the first snow of next winter. Kaja smiled at her husband, and Birul smiled back. Apmut remembered how it had been his own wife who won the alder stick contest the year before—and the prediction had come true, just as the shaman had said it would.

Soon, the summer would be here with its long days of constant light, its ripe, delicious berries, its Midnight Sun. There would be many things to enjoy—as well as a lot of work to be done. But many a man would, in the back of his mind, be waiting for something, a very special something in the changing Lappland seasons. Every real bear-hunter knew what it was. *The first fall of light snow, in early winter!*

32

The Lapp who cursed thunder

To the lovely region around Lyngen, on the coast of northern Norway, came two Lapp families every year. They came from Swedish Lappland, where they spent the winter keeping their reindeer in the mountains, down to the summer-pasture lands near the sea, where the reindeer moss was plentiful.

Twice a year they migrated back and forth, taking their tents with them, as nomadic reindeer-owners do. They took even their smallest children with them, including the babies in their cradles of hollowed-out birch-wood.

Now, amongst these children there was a little girl in one family, and a boy in the other, who were almost the same age. The little girl's name was Mari-Lyma Kitti, and the boy's name was Slunta Sarri. Sometimes they used to play together, but not as much as one might have thought, for Slunta was a bad-tempered boy who soon became quarrelsome, even with placid little Mari-Lyma. And sometimes they worked together, for there is so much work connected with having reindeer, especially two different herds that roam together and have to be separated for branding, counting, etc., that even the children have to help as much as they can.

The older Mari-Lyma and Slunta got, the more they were

able to help their parents: branding new calves, preparing the reindeer-skins for sewing into clothing, as well as looking for sennegrass to line their winter shoes with, beating it soft, and tying it up in thick strands for later use. And the older they got, the more bad-tempered Slunta became. He liked Mari-Lyma very much, but that didn't stop him quarrelling with her every time they were together. Mari-Lyma quite liked Slunta too, but then she was so sweet-natured that she liked everyone.

By the time the two of them were grown-up, their parents had begun to think that it would be a good idea to unite even further the Kitti and Sarri families, who had migrated together for so long, year-in and year-out, by marrying Mari-Lyma Kitti to Slunta Sarri. Mari-Lyma did not like the idea at all. But she did not know how to tell her parents this, because she knew how much it meant to them. And no Lapp girl likes to go against her parents' wishes.

Not even the fact that he might soon be engaged to Mari-Lyma seemed to make any difference to Slunta's temper. Quite the opposite, in fact. The slightest thing was enough to make him angry, and he began to curse violently every time anything crossed him. Poor Mari-Lyma did not know *what* to do! She had almost decided that she would have to disobey her parents (a *dreadful* thing for a Lapp girl to do), when something happened which was to solve the problem for her—in an awful and terrible way.

It was autumn, time to round-up the reindeer which had been roaming freely together all summer. Now they had to be collected together, and separated into two herds according to whether they had the Kitti brandmark or the Sarri brandmark on their ears. Every available person was needed for this, especially as some of the animals would have to be slaughtered to provide food and skins for clothing. All this work made autumn one of the busiest times of the year for reindeer owners.

Soon they discovered that some of their reindeer seemed to be missing. They must have strayed away from the main body of the herd, and wandered off on their own. When this happened, as it often did, somebody had to be sent to look for them. And this time, it was decided that Mari-Lyma and Slunta were the ones who could best be spared to do the searching. So they set off in the direction where it was most probable that they would find the missing reindeer.

For a long time they walked and walked, but could not find them. Slunta began to get angry, and to curse the missing animals. Then the weather started to change, as it can very rapidly in Lappland.

It had been pleasantly warm from the autumn sun, but now the warmth changed gradually to a heavy, sticky heat which warned of a coming storm. Mari-Lyma looked up, and saw how the storm-clouds were gathering, dark and low on the horizon. Slunta saw it too, and it made him so quarrelsome that he started to blame Mari-Lyma—first for the change in the weather, next for the fact that they couldn't find the reindeer. Mari-Lyma said nothing. She never did talk much, and now the black skies overhead and Slunta's equally black mood, frightened her into silence. She just kept on hoping that they might soon find the reindeer. And fortunately, they soon did.

The missing animals were half-way up a steeply-sloping incline, at the top of which was a wide, flat expanse. They were not grazing peacefully, but moving uneasily around, sensing the nearness of the storm from the heaviness in the air. And scarcely had Mari-Lyma and Slunta found the reindeer than the storm broke. There came a clap of thunder, as yet some distance away but near enough to frighten Mari-Lyma badly. She was not used to hearing it, for thunder and lightning are rare in Lappland, and the Lapps regarded them as very bad omens, a sign of anger in the Heavens. The reindeer too were frightened, so much so that they just huddled up close together and would not move from the place at the top of the incline which they had by now reached. It was no good Mari-Lyma and Slunta trying to drive them down and get them started on the way back to Lyngen. They just would not move from the spot.

Then came a second clap of thunder, much nearer than the first, followed by a flash of lightning. Slunta began to curse—first the reindeer, then Mari-Lyma, then the thunder and lightning. He swore and cursed for so long that Mari-Lyma became even more frightened of him than of the storm. She knew it was wicked to curse—and dangerous to curse the elements—for they might curse back, in their own way. Terror of what might happen if they did, at last gave her the courage to speak.

'Slunta, you must not curse the elements.' she warned him. 'It is very dangerous, especially when they are already angry, as now.'

But Slunta took no notice. He cursed the thunder again and again and said that, whoever it was who was making the thunder-noise, they belonged not up in the heavens, but down in the hot inferno below! At this there was a loud and angry roll of thunder, followed by a vivid f-l-a-s-h of lightning much, much closer than before.

'Slunta, do not curse the elements,' beseeched Mari-Lyma. 'If you go on like that, they *will* curse back at you.'

But Slunta just would not listen. 'The elements will do nothing to *me*,' he boasted. 'For I am stronger than they are. And if you like the thunder so much, you can go with it to the hot inferno below.'

There was no time for Mari-Lyma to speak to him again after that. For scarcely had Slunta finished speaking than a *terrible* roll of thunder erupted in the sky, immediately over their heads, so LOUD, and lasting so LONG, that Mari-Lyma thought it must surely have cleft the very earth. Utterly terrified, she flung herself flat on the ground, but nothing could shut out the many-forked flash of lightning which streaked angrily across the sky after the thunder, illuminating everything for hundreds of miles during the brief time it lasted.

For a long time after it had passed, Mari-Lyma lay still, except for her trembling. At last, scarcely daring to move, she looked up. The thunder and lightning had stopped. There was no sound, not even from the reindeer. Slunta too lay still. And then Mari-Lyma saw *why*. He had been struck by lightning. He and all his clothes were scorched right through. There was nothing she could do. She had done all she could when she warned him not to curse the elements, or they would curse back.

It took Mari-Lyma a long time, all on her own to collect the reindeer together and drive them down near Lyngen to where the other members of the Kitti and Sarri families had rounded-up the main part of the herd and fenced them in, in a special enclosure. They were surprised to see her return alone. The thunderstorm had swept over Lyngen too, and they had all lain, frightened, inside their tents, but the thunder and lightning had not been as bad as higher up, where Mari-Lyma came from. No one had been hurt.

Sadly, Mari-Lyma told them what had happened. She had to tell the whole story several times before they could really take in what had occurred. But when they at last understood, they agreed, just as sadly, that Slunta had deserved his punishment by the elements, for cursing them.

Later, both families returned to Swedish Lappland for the winter. And every year they continued their migrations together, back and forth between the mountains and the sea. And in the meantime, the rest of their children grew up. One day, several years later, one of Mari-Lyma's brothers married one of the Sarri girls, thus uniting even more closely the two nomadic families who had migrated together for so long. Their parents were very happy, and so was Mari-Lyma, who later found a much more suitable husband than Slunta would have been. But no one ever forgot the terrible story of what had happened to him.

And that is why, even today, no matter how much it may rain, nor how heavily the snow may fall, nor how wildly the wind may blow, nor, especially, how much thunder and lightning there may be, the Lapps still say, 'Never curse the elements! They are stronger than we are—and they might curse back!'